Flower Arranging in House and Garden

George Smith

Flower Arranging in House and Garden

George Smith

Drawings by Charles Stitt

Pelham Books
London

For Brian

First published in Great Britain by
PELHAM BOOKS LTD
44 Bedford Square
London WC1B 3DU
November 1977
Second Impression November 1978
Third Impression April 1979
Fourth Impression June 1981

ISBN 0 7207 0958 X

Printed and bound in Singapore
by Kyodo Shing Loong Printing Industries Pte. Ltd.

Contents

List of Illustrations

Acknowledgements

I wish to express my sincere gratitude to everyone who has assisted in any way towards this production. Most especially to my friend, Brian J. Withill, for his encouragement and help at all times and for typing the text.

My thanks to Charles Stitt of Matfield, Kent, for his beautiful line drawings, faithfully executed with painstaking care. Our collaboration together has been a source of pleasure to me based on our mutual love of plants. The excellence of his work speaks for itself.

My flower arrangements have been photographed by Tim Megson of Warren Jepson & Co. Ltd., of Leeds. He is responsible for Plates I, VI, VIII, X, XI, XII, XIII, XIV, XV. The remaining seven plates and the dust jacket are the work of Alex Marwood of York. I thank them both for their patience and skill.

Norman Puckering, my gardener, has produced almost all the flowers and foliage used in my decorations and I thank him for his unfailing help and loyalty. My grateful thanks, also, to Mrs Mary Wilson who has cared for and cherished the contents of this house, which create the setting for the arrangements.

Finally, I wish to thank Eric Marriott, Ruth Baldwin, John Elsegood and all the staff of Pelham Books Ltd., for their good-natured help and advice in the publication of this book.

Metric Conversion Table

$\frac{1}{2}$ in.	=	13 mm
1 in.	=	25 mm
2 in.	=	51 mm
3 in.	=	76 mm
5 in.	=	127 mm
6 in.	=	152 mm
7 in.	=	178 mm
8 in.	=	203 mm
9 in.	=	229 mm
10 in.	=	254 mm
11 in.	=	279 mm
1 ft	=	0·305 m
2 ft	=	0·610 m
3 ft	=	0·914 m
4 ft	=	1·219 m
5 ft	=	1·524 m
6 ft	=	1·828 m
7 ft	=	2·133 m
8 ft	=	2·438 m
9 ft	=	2·743 m
10 ft	=	3·043 m
11 ft	=	3·353 m
12 ft	=	3·658 m

Introduction

This book is about how to arrange flowers in the home and which plants to grow for cutting. It is written for everyone who appreciates the beauty of growing things, but with two particular groups of people in mind. First, the flower arrangers, who require a year-round supply of interesting plant material for picking and who want to know what to grow for their decorations. Second, it is for those people who wish to grow decorative and more permanent plant associations in their gardens. The line drawings and photographs are all designed to support the text in an effort to illustrate these two points of view. I find considerable pleasure and relaxation in both flower arranging and gardening and feel the two occupations are very inter-dependent. My hope is that this book will help to foster a greater harmony and understanding between those who gather and those who only grow. Perhaps the result will be a new hybrid, the arranger-gardener.

Ten years have elapsed since the publication of my first book, *Flower Arrangements and their Setting*, now out of print. This new work attempts to answer the many encouraging requests I have received during the intervening decade for a book on 'what to grow and how to arrange it'. Sixty plants are described, all useful for cutting and also for garden decoration. These raw materials of our art are illustrated with line drawings and discussed with cultural information based on twenty years of gardening experience and observation. The conditioning and the treatment of cut plant materials are fully explained, together with the after-care of the ingredients of an arrangement. I am conscious that this is only a small personal selection but faced with so much choice I am forced to limit myself to those I consider essential.

The construction of the flower arrangements is fully explained, great stress being placed on the mechanical support and the various types of foundation employed for this purpose. The photographic plates illustrate the finished creations; all are designed to accord with my home and they span one year's growth. As in my previous book, considerable emphasis is placed on the background and setting to show how much these influence our choice of flowers, foliage, containers and accessories. The importance of colour blending is discussed together with the harmony that can be achieved by the right combination of forms and textures, complementary to their surroundings. The jargon of the flower arranger is expressed in simple terms in the hope that the novice may find help and encouragement. There are also ideas for the more experienced decorator who seeks fresh inspiration. There are many basic principles laid down in all art forms, but these are not categorically stated here. I feel that the best flower arrangers are those who learn to develop their own natural talents uninhibited by too many rules. To arrange our gardens and flowers as we please is one of the few remaining forms of self-expression left to us, in a world preoccupied with conformity and standardization.

As each season unfolds I will describe favourite plants recommended for inclusion in the arranger's garden. I write only of those I know and grow, very conscious of the fact that one never stops learning and not wishing to set myself up as a horticultural pundit. Most are well known, but I do not hesitate to include them just because they are plentiful, for this is an eclectic collection. A few are rare and will require some searching for and it is for this reason I have included a list, by no means exhaustive, of sympathetic stockists in Britain. Many flower and garden friends have furnished the bulk of my collection over the years and I remember them with gratitude. 'Admire to acquire' is a somewhat avaricious maxim, but certainly it works, for the true gardener is generous with both cuttings and information. There is also the canny wisdom that a plant banked with a friend can be useful stock if the original fails; forgive me if that sounds a little calculating.

Text without illustration becomes a dull affair and I am sincerely grateful to Charles Stitt for gracing these pages with his sensitive drawings. Almost all the plants were drawn from live specimens, picked by him in my garden. Through his eyes I have seen new beauty and become even more aware of the perceptive ability of the artist to see a plant as a living work of art. His skill as a draughtsman, attention to detail and faithfulness to his subject abundantly prove his love of plants. Black and white line drawings convey a better impression of the sixty plants selected than monochrome photographs might have done in the same space, as well as adding enormously to the decorative quality of the book, for his drawings are arrangements in themselves. In most cases the emphasis has been placed on leaves, for it is these that the arranger most needs, but that is not to say that I do not recommend their flowers also.

Garden flowers and foliage form the basis of my designs as a lecturer-demonstrator and I am fortunate that my travels in Britain give me the opportunity to seek out plants for this purpose. My visits to many overseas countries enable me to absorb ideas which can later be adapted with less exotic vegetation. I do not grow solely for the purpose of cutting, but with an eye to planting a group as a living arrangement. All too often the average garden is a haphazard affair, lacking any thoughtful planning and cohesion. For those of you who prefer to leave your flowers growing I include suggestions for plant associations which will enliven your garden by the juxtaposition of varied leaf forms, unusual flowers and fascinating seedheads. This type of planting is the underlying theme of the garden at Heslington. Here I have been twice blessed. First, to have continued in a garden already profusely stocked by Nina, Lady Deramore, a discerning gardener, who with the added guidance of Mr Graham Stuart Thomas, a plantsman of immense knowledge and taste, created from a derelict farmstead a garden with charm and character. Second, and possibly most fortuitous of all, has been the continuing good service of Mr Norman Puckering, most loyal and understanding of gardeners, without whom there would be no garden upon which to base this book.

Why arrange flowers at all, why not leave them growing? This question asked by the sceptical is hard to answer completely. In each one of us, in varying degrees, rises the desire to be creative and flower arranging is one of the activities which enables us to fulfil this urge. To paint with flowers is our aim and to express through a living, three-dimensional medium our enjoyment of growing things. We cannot live without plants to maintain the balance of our environment. They purify the atmosphere and provide food for ourselves and our animals. Yet one indefinable need still remains, that which appeals to our aesthetic senses. This is well delineated in the Chinese proverb: 'If you have two loaves, sell one, and with that coin buy a lily; for the first loaf will feed the body, but the lily will feed the soul'. Of course if you have only one loaf you have a problem, but if you have no soul, read no further.

1 Winter

Winter offers a challenge to the flower arranger; it is the dormant season when we plan ahead and review the year past. There are flowers and leaves to be found outdoors more precious for their scarcity. Cutting them enables them to develop in warm rooms and affords us the opportunity to inspect them at closer quarters together with the enjoyment of elusive fragrances. Many early spring flowers bought from the florist lack good foliage, but with the help of winter-flowering shrubs and evergreen leaves we can make them go a little further.

Three perennial plants of contrasting form appear in Figure 1. They say at once something which will be repeated again and again: form, colour and texture. To be aware of these and to employ them is to begin to be an artist with plant material. First, form: look at the way the tall, sweeping curve of the ruscus contrasts with the solid, round leaf of the bergenia which in turn appears more solid because of the small, scalloped leaf of the tellima. Their colour we cannot see, but experience will tell us they are all green in varying values or strengths. Their texture, the tactile surface, is smooth and shiny in the ruscus, mat, smooth and leathery in the bergenia, and rough and hispid in the case of the tellima. Already we know something about these leaves, we can see them and mentally we can feel them. These are qualities which begin to add to our appreciation. We may not know how to grow or arrange them, but we are aware of them. Awareness is the first step, observation supported by experience. When we make an arrangement indoors or plant a group outdoors we shall employ these three qualities and at the risk of being didactic I have laboured them, frequently employed without analysis. It is the individual qualities of our raw materials which add up to the success or otherwise of the completed design.

As this is also a gardening book, cultural notes accompany each plant illustrated, with a few additional species or varieties offered as alternatives. A plant appreciated by Gertrude Jekyll, the mother of modern gardening, is *Bergenia cordifolia*, which seems to be either loved or detested. Graham Thomas calls it 'a godsend – invaluable as a contrast for vases indoors': what more can we ask? Sybil Emberton states, 'One of the indispensable "props" of the flower arrangement – lasts almost interminably in water': there is another eulogistic opinion. Christopher Lloyd, on the other hand, 'loathes' the plant and finds it 'boring at best and really dreadful at [its] worst'. As always, he has a point, for, overplanted in thick mats, bergenia can be dull, with flowers of almost toothpaste pink on rhubarb-red stems. Despite all this, nothing fills the bill quite so easily, is so long-suffering, weed-proof and pest-free. The best forms of *Bergenia cordifolia* are a liverish red in winter; others turn the odd leaf amber and scarlet in autumn. I have one which always produces a neat, red margin to each leaf in hot, dry weather. Look out for a good form from this variable species. Bergenias come from Siberia so they know better than to complain, growing and colouring best in exposed, not over-rich soil. A garden hybrid received from the late Margery Fish and raised in Ireland is 'Ballawley' with large, reflexed, shining leaves, green in summer turning to raw meat-red in two tones in winter. The striking flowers, which are clear magenta and on long, red stems, are sometimes caught by April frost. It appreciates a sheltered site and richer soil.

For a small, spoon-shaped leaf *Bergenia purpurascens* takes the prize in winter, when its erect stance and ox-blood-red colour combine well with Christmas Roses and snowdrops. 'Sunningdale' has yet to prove its claim to be more colourful: bigger it certainly is. Soil and aspect influence their appearance considerably. I have a washy pink-flowered variety which produces burnished, copper leaves ideal for picking in January and February. It grows on a clay bank in full light but on sheltered loam remains all green, so try moving it about.

Soft ruscus, a commercially imported foliage, belongs in the indestructible category as cut material. Yet it is rarely seen in gardens as *Danaë racemosa*. Legend says Alexander the Great was crowned with this pliant and enduring evergreen. It is a native of the eastern Mediterranean and named in honour of Danaë, daughter of King Acrisius of Argos. Because of its origins the Alexandrian Laurel has a reputation for tenderness, but I find it hardy and long-suffering. It is a slow-growing plant but given shelter and moisture it will slowly increase by underground shoots, throwing up long, green stems. I have used it in France in four-foot wands, but mine are only half this size in a Yorkshire garden. The side stems are clothed with shiny, elliptical, green leaves. Technically speaking, these are modified stems called 'cladodes'. I mention this only because I suspect it could live in drier, scrubbier conditions as it loses little by way of transpiration. It is the only member of its family or genus, which must make its life uncomplicated. Nevertheless, this graceful plant is sometimes confused with its stiff-stemmed relative, the prickly *Ruscus aculeatus* or Butcher's Broom. The entire stem preserves well by the process described in Chapter 7, turning pale honey in colour and lasting indefinitely.

The third plant in Figure 1 is an easy charmer, ideal for small shady gardens. *Tellima grandiflora* has no well known common name or I would include it. Botanical Latin names may appear irritating to the layman and are not used here merely in an attempt to appear learned. They tell us much about a plant, have international recognition and are acceptable parlance to gardeners of all nationalities. Vernacular names vary from one country to another and even more locally and they can, therefore, be misleading. Tellima is an anagram of mitella, a genus which it closely resembles, and both are similar to the tiarellas. They all enjoy

moist, woodland conditions, forming low-growing clumps. The leaves of tellima are prettily scalloped and rounded, and up to five inches across but usually less. The main feature is the network of bronze veins, most pronounced on new leaves in winter. Propagate by division as self-sown progeny are not always well marked. The slender stems of flowers, or racemes, are threaded with nodding, green bells fringed with pink and appearing in May like elongated Lilies-of-the-Valley. They last cut if mature, but dislike water-retaining foams. In winter the foliage will last up to a month in water and should be cut rather than pulled in order to sever the strong thread-like veins. The purple-leaved form, *T. grandiflora* 'Purpurea', is indistinguishable in summer but turns beetroot red in winter.

Planted together, the three plants shown in Figure 1 would create a pleasing combination, being compatible as to soil and site requirements. Once we start to consider the association of one plant with another and to understand their cultural needs and growth habits we are a long way towards creating better flower arrangements. Just as in the garden the soil-type and the site will dictate the planting, so indoors the flower arrangement will be governed by its setting. Constance Spry called this 'suitability'. She had an innate sense of it. This highly tuned feeling for what to put with what, sometimes called flair, is a rare gift, not given to us all in the same degree. However, this degree can be developed by example, exposure to the right environment and an ability to practise constantly. The true artist is never satisfied.

Flower arranging has developed considerably since the time of Mrs Spry, yet many of her maxims hold good, the chief of these being 'When in doubt leave it out'. We revere her memory, acknowledging that she created her own style for a wealthy and discerning clientele. Few of us have the opportunity to arrange in the grand manner, yet we can still strive towards individuality and originality. Knowing what style to choose for a particular setting is a matter of practice, which in time becomes instinctive,

Figure 1

Danaë racemosa

Bergenia cordifolia

Tellima grandiflora

enabling us to select the right flowers, vase and position for every occasion.

Now for some simple guidance about making arrangements intended only for the novice. First, a word about vases – usually referred to as containers. A container may be anything so long as it is functional, attractive and water-tight. Avoid over-decorated surfaces as they are distracting. A container need not be expensive or elaborate and should never be selected with these criteria in mind. Obviously a beautiful vase will enhance choice flowers, but it should be subordinate to them, in harmony and scale with its surroundings. A good collection of containers takes time to acquire and the days of junk-shop bargains are mostly past. Simple shapes, classical or modern, in neutral colours and with quality of manufacture, are worth looking out for. A hand-made object will always take preference because it already possesses individuality. Studio pottery, basketry, antique metal, alabaster and wood are all sympathetic surfaces to plant material. Cut-glass and crystal are rarely effective as they show a mass of stems and the support.

The devices used to hold stems in place are called collectively 'mechanics', a much used word in the flower arranger's vocabulary. The cheapest and most useful, especially for thick stems, is still wire netting. Purchased from ironmongers, it should be of two-inch mesh and eighteen-gauge thickness. Crumpling the wire to fit the vase will reduce the diameter of the holes and the amount required is a matter of personal preference. Cut ends left upstanding are useful to attach over the container rim and to twist around wayward branches. Never make the mistake of using fine mesh as once it becomes crumpled it is impassable to all but the finest stems. Plastic-coated wire is less pliable to fix and not easy to hide.

A pinholder, a lead base set with closely packed brass pins, is useful for anchoring material in a shallow dish and much favoured by exponents of Japanese flower arranging or Ikebana; it is known as a needlepoint holder in the United States of America. It makes a useful stabilizer when used in conjunction with wire netting. Secure with Plasticine or floral clay to the bottom surface of the container when all items are dry. Three small pills of fixative should ensure a firm union. Pinholders for use with floral foam consist of a lead base fitted with about six longer prongs and are used as ballast.

Water-retaining foams, the most universally known being Oasis, consist of a green, plastic material which rapidly absorbs water. One standard block will soak up as much as three pints of water and its use has revolutionized our art. Cut a piece to fit the container and then float the block on a basin of water until it sinks: this should take no more than ten minutes. Place in the container and strap in place with green adhesive tape, sold for this purpose by florists. Crumbling of the foam only results if it has been over-soaked or overloaded. Part-used foam should be stored in a plastic bag as it is difficult to resoak once dry. It can be used several times but should not be relied upon for thick stems after the first using. As it has a slight grain to it, it is usually easier to insert cut stems into the top of a block rather than the sides though both will be used when the block projects above the rim.

Whatever type of support you may choose, and it will vary according to container and purpose, try to ensure complete stability before embarking on the design. There is nothing more unnerving to novice and expert alike if things cannot be relied upon to stay put. Short cuts with mechanics rarely pay off and a collapsed arrangement is usually the result of inadequate preparation. I find many beginners are unfair to themselves in the matter of tools. Blunt knives, slack snippers and rusty scissors are twice as difficult to work with and hinder progress towards proficiency. With the right equipment for the job, not only will your efforts proceed more efficiently but you will acquire skill and dexterity much more quickly. The paraphernalia of the flower arranger can become legion: watering-can, dust sheets, spare wires, sticky tape and many other items have a habit of losing

themselves, so a basket to keep them all together can be useful.

Whilst still on basic matters may I warn against the accumulation of too many 'props'. It is a great temptation to collect all kinds of accessories, drapery and the like, which 'might just come in handy', or so we tell ourselves. Fortunately the trend is away from the nick-nackery of the past decades, greater emphasis now being placed on plant material and less on the supporting items. Natural objects will always harmonize well with plant material but that Spanish doll which looked so tempting in Costa Whatnot is best forgotten. As a judge of competitive exhibits I am constantly assailed by a bewildering assortment of objects included by the competitor in an effort to convey to me, and the general public, the theme of their choice. As this book is about flowers in the home, I shall try to spare you such inclusions.

Having decided to cut our flowers or foliage there arises the question of how best to keep them alive. The process known as conditioning is of paramount importance and is a laborious operation that cannot be skipped. Throughout the book I have included instructions appertaining to individual items, but here are a few general points for guidance.

Gathering should be done early in the morning whilst the plant is still charged with moisture, or failing this in the evening. Take the bucket to the plant where possible. Remove surplus leaves, crush or split open woody stems or pare away two inches of bark and any thorns with a knife. Stand in deep water. Hot or warm water has miraculous restorative powers for flagging material. Certain tricky subjects can be conditioned by boiling for one minute, stem ends only. Fill an old pan, reserved for the purpose, with boiling water, wrap all parts other than the stem ends in a cloth or paper to protect them from steam. Place the cut ends into the boiling water for one to two minutes and then reimmerse in deep, tepid water. This sounds drastic, but it works wonders with immature growth and temperamental subjects. Stems

which exude a sap or milky latex should be singed in a flame. Dipping in dry soil will stem the flow until they can be properly treated. Total immersion is beneficial to large leaves and sprays of foliage, but over-long soaking may spoil their texture. Obviously woolly or furry textured stems and leaves need special care. Try to wipe away excess felt or hairs and condition in shallow water after boiling cut ends. Many grey subjects resent plastic foam and will syphon water if over-wet. Recutting any stem under water helps to relieve an air lock and is recommended for stems with central threads, such as tellima. The more mature the growth, the easier it will be to condition, provided it is still in its prime. Material being conditioned should be kept in a cool, dark, airy place and allowed to drink deeply for up to twelve hours. This initial attention will greatly extend the life of our raw materials. There are no short cuts to this process, which in the end repays the effort. Bought flowers should have already been conditioned, but recutting the stems and a long drink are still advisable.

Construct your arrangement where it is to stand. It is absolutely fatal to create a decoration at one table level and then move it to a higher or lower position. Arranging *in situ* is my one and only golden rule and I have applied it even on the most valuable pieces of furniture. The angle at which we view the finished arrangement will vary, so it pays to sit down or stand back occasionally, to study these angles. This arty, head-on-one-side stance of the flower arranger can be developed into quite a performance when burlesqued by the non-flower arranger.

The arrangement in Plate I is a prelude to the many wonderful flowers that will unfold as the year progresses. The container is a handsome pewter platter contemporary with the seventeenth-century oak chest. The grey pewter and the dark oak have a sombre strength suggestive of winter; the background is kept deliberately free of distractions. All these elements set the scene and the arranger should consider the setting before anything else. As the

II Tropical foliage with green flowers

chest is lower than the average table, we get the impression of looking downwards as if on to a garden. This low position dictates a natural style well suited to short-stemmed winter flowers.

One branch of *Mahonia japonica* gives a sparse windswept first placement, impaled on a big pinholder placed at the back of a bowl used to line the platter. I would never put wet foam or water in direct contact with the surface of the plate as this would spoil its patina. The flowers include growing clumps of yellow *Iris danfordiae*, cut stems of Christmas Roses, *Helleborus niger* 'Potter's Wheel', white freesia, daffodils and paper-white narcissi. The cut items are all in separate glass tubes or plastic cornets as many of them dislike water-retaining foam. Carpet moss and bun moss are used to conceal the block of Oasis which holds the cut foliage. This consists of the golden-green *Elaeagnus pungens* 'Maculata', *Bergenia* 'Ballawley' and *Bergenia purpurascens*, together with two evergreen ferns described in the final chapter. Winter-flowering shrubs are especially welcome and catkins of *Garrya elliptica* can be seen on the lower right, together with sprays of winter-flowering jasmine, *Jasminum nudiflorum*. The interesting point about this decoration is the inclusion of pot plants to give extra interest. The white cyclamen and iris bulbs are still on their roots and in this way last much longer. Detailed instructions on how to make a dish or plate garden are given in Chapter 2.

The after-care of any arrangement is important. This means a daily topping up of all decorations with a long-spouted watering-can. Central heating and hot, smoky atmospheres spell death to flowers. A gentle over-head syringe of water will prove most beneficial, especially for delicate ferns and young spring greenery, provided adequate precautions are taken to protect the furniture. Where this is not practicable, a thin veil of polythene can be placed over the flowers at night to help conserve humidity. Draughts either of cold or, worse still, of hot air will cause even well conditioned material to flag. Just as plants seem to respond to

some people and not to others, so it is with cut flowers. Gardeners call this 'green thumb' or 'green fingers', but it boils down to the fact that some people take pains whilst others do not trouble. The length of time flowers will live will be governed by many factors, but if the initial conditioning is not properly done, then the arranger is destined for disappointment. Changing the water daily is unnecessary and often impractical for arranged flowers. To remove flowers from a hot room at night into a cool, moist atmosphere will certainly help them to live longer.

Evergreen shrubs provide the arranger with long-lasting foliage for cutting as well as furnishing the garden in winter. Three of the most useful are illustrated in Figure 2. It has been said that great beauty in a woman begins with the right bone structure and this is also true of gardens. For unless they are designed with some permanent features they become uninteresting during the dormant season. Evergreens give to the garden its bone structure, the deciduous plants may be the flesh, flowers mere cosmetics. One shrub coveted for its size by my garden visitors is *Elaeagnus pungens* 'Maculata', a slow starter but a shrub which will eventually make rapid growth when established. Grown in full sunlight, few shrubs can compare with the splash of winter sunshine it gives to the garden. Resist the temptation to pick it too young as hard picking will ruin its basic outline. The dark green, oval leaves are generously splashed and streaked with yellow, silver on the reverse. They are carried on rather stiff, angular branches and it is only inside an established bush that the curvaceous sprays we desire are to be found. Occasionally it puts out an all-green reverted shoot which should be removed on sight. Cut foliage lasts several weeks in water if picked mature; never pick the young bronze leaves which take all summer to develop. It can be preserved with glycerine, but is preferable in the natural state. Much more useful for this purpose is *Elaeagnus macrophylla*, with all-green leaves with a silvery reverse which is retained

Figure 2

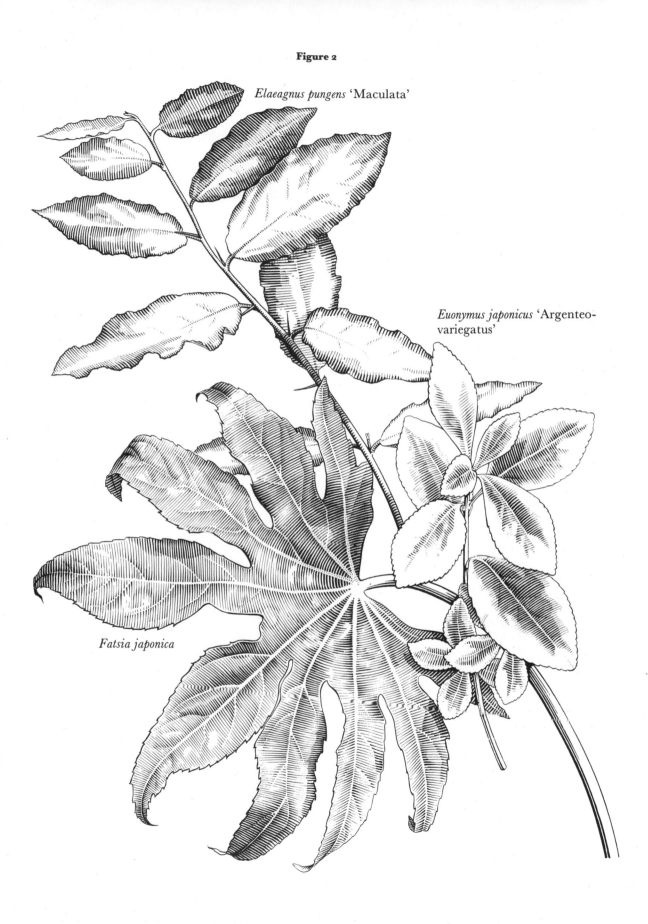

Elaeagnus pungens 'Maculata'

Euonymus japonicus 'Argenteo-
variegatus'

Fatsia japonica

whilst the upper surface changes to a soft parchment brown.

The next shrub is less frequently met with and should not be confused with more lowly relatives. *Euonymus japonicus* 'Argenteo-variegatus' grows up to six feet tall and has much larger leaves, margined with white, overlaid with grey-green towards the centre, and is bigger in every way than *Euonymus fortunei*. It needs a sheltered corner and mine is espaliered against a brick wall in the lee of the house where it can be enjoyed through a circular window. Unlike *Euonymus fortunei* it does not produce aerial roots for climbing or any cold-weather pink tinges. The new spring growth is lime green edged with cream in striking contrast to the previous year's growth, not unlike the bushy, golden forms of *Euonymus japonicus*. This is a plant worth searching for and lasts a long time as cut material. Like all heavily variegated plants it requires green companions to show it to advantage, for too many variegations tend to cancel each other out.

Fatsia japonica has the boldest of all outdoor leaves in Britain. It is erroneously known as Castor Oil Plant, which is in fact *Ricinus communis*. As a pot plant it is occasionally met with forlornly residing in fishmonger's windows. Even outdoors *Fatsia japonica* spreads handsome leaves with a sub-tropical, self-conscious air, as if caught straying from the greenhouse. Once settled, it associates well with masonry preferring the shelter of a wall or building. The tough leaves are palmate, nine-pointed on long leaf-stalks, glossy when young, more leathery and finely veined when ageing. They make handsome focal material for large groups and have dramatic appeal in modern designs. Although long-lasting when cut, they have an irritating habit of flopping forward unless gently massaged. By midsummer lower leaves discolour and turn yellow and black. Once removed from the plant, which looks better for the grooming, they are attractive additions to arrangements of fruit. Glycerining the leaves – details in Chapter 7 – requires time and patience, for unless the leaves are propped upright this tendency to fall forward will prevent the solution from reaching all portions. A fully cured leaf is a thing of beauty and utility, lasting indefinitely, like well polished leather. The variegated form cannot be relied upon outside. A cross between the Irish ivy, *Hedera hibernica*, and *Fatsia japonica* has given us x *Fatshedera lizei*, more frequently met as a house plant. I grow it trained up a wall which offers some protection, encouraging it to flower and bear green-black fruits in mild winters.

The arrangement of tropical foliage and green flowers in Plate II will appeal to those who prefer the classical style. I realize not everyone has access to such exotic vegetation, but a similar effect could be achieved with more homely ingredients. The elegant palm and colourful croton leaves, *Codiaeum variegatum pictum*, were gathered in Bermuda, a flower arranger's paradise. Sprays of elaeagnus and danaë could be used to create the same sweeping lines, if less flamboyantly, with tinted bergenias to replace the croton. Having such beautiful foliage I naturally wished to use it to the maximum effect and to incorporate two varieties of euphorbia described in Chapter 2. The four central flower heads, known botanically as cyathia, are of 'Lambrook Lime', whilst the two more solid ones right and left show the maroon eye of *Euphorbia characias*. Many synonyms are used for these spurges with a tangle of specific epithets. I have based my researches on the Royal Horticultural Society's *Dictionary of Gardening* (second edition) and its supplement in an effort to be as up to date as possible in the changing world of plant nomenclature. I hope that my readers will not close their minds to the use of correct botanical names for reasons already explained. Other plant material includes the ever-popular variegated aspidistra, clipped Chinese fan palms and glycerined fronds of leather fern. Central rosettes of *Echeveria rosea* pick up the curtain colour. This Mexican succulent, picked from the greenhouse, blooms in February and March and has pink leaves and stems which set off the acid yellow flowers.

The colour-scheme of the room, style of furnishing and occasion for which the arrangement will be used should all be considered before selecting the vase. In Plate II the classical French urn of Sienese marble and ormolu filled with Oasis is heavy enough to support this airy triangular design. It stands on a French Empire mahogany writing table whose green leather top relates in colour to the carpet and pelmet trim. The height of the decoration is balanced by the legs and curved base of the desk, with the arch and alcove mirror adding a sense of depth; the arrangement is lit by the window on the left. All these factors add up to a harmonious composition, created *in situ*, the most important being a sense of scale. All too often we see beautiful flowers chopped down to conform to some arbitrary rule established as a flexible guide but too frequently slavishly applied. That is why I prefer to teach by example, for guiding principles we may need as a discipline, but personal experience and constant practice are still the best masters.

2 Spring

Spring flowers and foliage are a welcome symbol of renewed life as winter gives way to warmer days and increasing daylight awakens many bulbs. Trees and shrubs await these first encouraging days to set in motion their growth cycle. Nature begins to unfold all the intricacies of her procreation after a period of rest. This change is evident in all forms of life, especially amongst birds whose dawn chorus becomes more insistent as territorial boundaries are established and the desire to find a mate is instinctively aroused. This change varies from one spring to the next and entirely depends on the sun, whose warmth and radiance governs all these manifestations. The first crocus still evokes in us a thrill at these hidden miracles.

One family of plants which act as an indicator of spring is the euphorbias. This is a genus of widely varied species including such diverse plants as our Christmas poinsettia and the barbarous Crown of Thorns. The hardy euphorbias of our gardens are a generous group giving colour and decoration for at least three months of the year in flower, plus attractive winter foliage and summer seedheads. Some put on a brief show of autumn colour, especially *Euphorbia dulcis* and *Euphorbia griffithii*. Three are illustrated in Figure 3. The first is useful as a specimen in association with masonry and prostrate plants. A simple yet striking combination would be *Euphorbia characias* with the lovely *Juniperus depressus* 'Bar Harbour', perhaps with the inclusion of a bergenia for three contrasting forms. There is a superb example of this prostrate evergreen juniper growing over a flat rock at Harlow Car Gardens near Harrogate, the headquarters of the Northern Horticultural Society. It is a pewter-bronze in winter, changing in spring to a soft celadon green.

Many names surround the least hardy of the three illustrated, but *Euphorbia characias wulfenii* first came to me as a gift from Mrs Margery Fish, a gardener tolerant of flower arrangers, if not herself one. I used to delight in my visits to her at East Lambrook Manor where her house, garden and personality formed such a pleasing and composite whole. Her apparent casualness put one completely at ease as she kept up a running commentary about the plants she grew and loved with almost maternal affection. How I regret I did not pay better attention to the pearls of knowledge she cast in all directions. 'Don't look at m'deads,' she would say as I eyed her massed collections of dried seedheads stuffed at random into pewter jugs. My quizzical glance she mistook for critical disapproval. I little realized I was in the presence of one of the great gardeners of this century, whose knowledge and skill would live on in her books and in the plants she so generously bestowed upon others. 'I shall have to charge you half-a-crown for this,' she said with an apologetic air as she produced some seedling treasure. 'Found it in the nursery bed.' Anything growing in the garden she was liable to break off or dig up free of charge, but nursery stock had to be paid for and this I respected. Looking back I realize she was helping to propagate much more than plants, she was also engendering something of herself. These truly generous folk are all too few.

Euphorbia characias comes from the hot, stony hillsides of the western Mediterranean; an arid setting suits it best, although it will grow taller in sheltered shade. The handsome evergreen foliage of soft blue-green extends like a bottle brush up the stem ending in clusters of inconspicuous green flowers. Each flower is surrounded by striking yellow-green bracts which last for many weeks as the main attraction. The central eye of the flower is maroon-red or brown. In the sub-species *Euphorbia characias wulfenii* the maroon eye is absent, and in the selected form 'Lambrook Lime' the whole appearance is more vivid chartreuse-green. I am persisting in calling it

'Lambrook Lime' rather than 'Lambrook Yellow', the name under which I see it listed, because this is the name with which Mrs Fish gave it to me. During frosty weather the plant looks dejected, the leaves compacted to the stem, the head turned over, rimmed with frost. As spring approaches and the crozier-like head extends and takes on a pink tinge, the plant is already beautiful. The arrival of spring can be considered complete by the appearance of the upright flower heads neatly arranged in terminal cyathia on three-foot stems. The seed capsules, which follow after three months of beauty, explode in hot weather accompanied by a cracking sound. The seeds are thrown many feet and often germinate in the most inhospitable crevices. After this the whole stem dies and should be removed at ground level. New growth will already be appearing from the base, growing on to clothe the shrub throughout the next winter.

As cut material this euphorbia will last for several weeks in water, but is less tolerant of water-retaining foams. Several heads appear in Plate II grouped with other greens. One note of caution applies to all euphorbias. The common name, Milkweed, comes from the sticky latex exuded when they are cut or damaged. This juice can cause inflammation and irritation to sensitive skins, especially around the eyes or mouth. Singe cut ends in a flame and wash your hands after the process.

There are at least sixteen euphorbias worthy of the garden so rather than make this read like a catalogue, I must content myself with only three for my choice, although others jostle for inclusion. *Euphorbia griffithii* is a sub-alpine plant from the East Himalayas. It grows almost four feet high and emerges in fits and starts from advancing underground shoots. These appear in March, a striking pink and green, developing into compact orange-red flowers with the characteristic bracts of the same orange red, the effect being more marked in the form called 'Fireglow'. The flower head expands and is extended by many side shoots, the whole cyathium paling to apricot as it ages. In October the plant turns to a golden yellow, every leaf edged with scarlet, a brilliant autumnal effect worth waiting for. It grows best in full sun with deep moist soil for full development. As cut material it is not so easy to condition, being rather soft in the early stages; singe and soak in deep water.

Perhaps the easiest of the three and certainly the most useful is *Euphorbia robbiae*. Never a nuisance, it is like an improved wood spurge getting on quietly with its job and is useful for ten months of the year. Hailing from Asia Minor, there is a charming story attributed to its discovery. It was collected in the wild near Istanbul by one of those intrepid lady botanists, Mrs Robb. She had reached the point on her expedition where all her vasculum tins were overflowing with specimens when she discovered this new species. She was armed with a stout hat box in which she kept her best hat worn only for impressing local dignitaries at border posts, to effect a smooth passage through dangerous territories. A difficult feminine decision faced her, whether to abandon the hat or the plant. Luckily for us the plant won and her sacrifice is perpetuated by the name 'Mrs Robb's Bonnet'.

After all this build-up you must be expecting something special, which I cannot claim it to be. Most experts dismiss it as ground cover, that all-embracing term for anything easy and rampant. Granted it can be both of these, but so much more besides. In winter compact rosettes of dark green leaves on nine-inch stems provide ideal material for the centre of a green arrangement. By early March these lengthen to arched flower spikes with lime-green buds. Pink leaflets surround the newly extended stem. The flower heads open in April to a vivid lime, holding this colour and our attention for a month or more. By June these have darkened to green and bronze, which in a hot, dry position eventually dries to biscuit brown in July or August. When these are cut away, a whole new crop of rosettes will be ready to fill the gap. Useful at any stage, condition as the others mentioned.

Plate III shows a small collection of spring flowers made for a guest bedroom. They create a welcome to be enjoyed at close quarters, arranged in a natural style as if growing. As many of these small, bulbous subjects lack foliage, this simple style helps to create the impression of a small garden with the flowers forcing their way out of the ground making a spontaneous and unlaboured design. The container is a sturdy octagonal bowl with a matt brown exterior glaze and a soft grey-green interior, pleasing even when empty. This colouring prompts the use of lichen-covered larch twigs for the outline. These are fixed on to a large pinholder placed about two-thirds of the way back in the bowl. The ground cover is of celadon green reindeer moss, described in Chapter 4. This loofah-like moss supports the leaves and flowers over wire netting lining the bowl.

The flowers are all chosen for their delicate colouring in a complementary scheme of pale lemon yellow contrasting with a soft violet-blue, cream variegated foliage and grey moss adding a neutral note. All the colour values are light which helps to increase the feeling of freshness and youth the arrangement should convey. Three varieties of narcissi form the tallest placements: on the left are the dainty, clustered flowers of *Narcissus x* 'Silver Chimes', a hybrid between the Angel's Tears or Triandrus group and the clustered Tazetta group. With this parentage we get the reflexed petal and long trumpet of the former combined with the bunch-flowered habit of the latter. The creamy white petals and soft yellow trumpet create a flower of distinction which grows paler as it develops. The central narcissi are 'Primrose Cheerfulness', a reliable garden variety. On the extreme right are the dainty, deeper yellow jonquils, *Narcissus juncifolius*, with a heavy scent like a gardenia – remarkably strong for such a small flower. Between these stand the nodding white bells of *Leucojum aestivum*, misleadingly called the Summer Snowflake, which flowers from mid-April to early May. The pendant white bells are

tipped with green on all six segments and stand on long, wiry stems, lovely in the garden or for arranging. Small species tulips have great attraction and the hybrids bearing the parentage of *Tulipa greigii* and *Tulipa kaufmanniana* often have the added attraction of leaves mottled and streaked with mauvish purple on a glaucous base, together with flowers of short stature whose slender, pointed petals reflex in the sunshine. These are often sold as Peacock mixtures and these blooms are 'The First', ivory white with a yellow base flushed with red outside. Another very dainty tulip is the star-like *Tulipa turkestanica* with up to five flowers per stem, white and cream with green markings, set off by purplish-brown anthers. The seedheads that follow are also desirable.

The central flowers are all from the primula family and include the fragrant violet-blue and dark purple old fashioned auricula. This once popular garden plant still has its enthusiasts and is often depicted in old flower paintings. Clusters of polyanthus form the focal point with two heads of *Primula denticulata* for contrast of colour. Close to the centre are the pale blue star-like flowers of *Ipheion uniflorum*, a native of South America and easily grown in a sunny, well drained border. On the extreme right can be seen the creamy bells of Dog's Tooth Violet, a graceful flower like a small reflexed-petal lily. The erythroniums are for shady, moist places where they will increase slowly, always surprising us with their fragile beauty and lovely marbled leaves. They mostly originate from North America. Below these in the illustration are a few sprays of a double-flowered jasmine grown from a cutting collected in Malta and surviving against a sheltered south wall.

The lowest placement is of *Clematis alpina* 'Columbine', an enchanting climber with delicate flowers of soft violet-blue, the colour of kittens' eyes, borne singly and set off by ferny green foliage. The seedheads which follow in summer are silky green at first, drying to whispy balls of grey – lovely for dried decorations if preserved with a gentle spray of hair lacquer.

Euphorbia charracias wulfenii 'Lambrook
Lime'

Figure 3

Euphorbia griffithii 'Fireglow'

Euphorbia robbiae

This same colouring is repeated on the left by flowers of *Anemone apennina*, a flower of open woodland, naturalizing most beautifully with other wild flowers. The central placement of pansies, combining both violet and yellow, help to fuse the entire colour-scheme. A few leaves of cardoon add their grey-green substance on the left to balance the frontal placement of *Astrantia major* 'Sunningdale Variegated', a plant of distinction illustrated in Figure 8 and described in Chapter 3.

A labour-saving way of arranging small spring flowers is to create a dish garden on the following lines. Select a large, water-proof tray, dish, or old fashioned meat platter and fix to this, with Plasticine, small two-inch test tubes (preferably flat-bottomed), small medicine bottles, plastic phials, or whatever comes to hand. A larger dish and pinholder can be placed at the back to take taller branches of early forced blossom or leafy twigs. Fill in between all the containers with moss so as to conceal them but taking care not to allow strands of moss to get into the tubes, for they will quickly empty them by a syphoning action. Small ferns, ivy trails and stones can also be included to create a natural effect. The whole design is now ready to receive whatever flowers and leaves are available. Group a few of one type in each bottle or tube, depending on their size and colour. As so many of these early spring bulbous subjects have weak stems and are too fragile to arrange in Oasis, or even wire netting, it is an ideal way of creating a very colourful alpine meadow indoors. Daily topping-up with water in each tube will keep it fresh for many weeks and moisten the moss in the process. On no account must the actual dish be flooded or the whole thing will become stagnant and smell unpleasant. The constantly changing pattern of flowers will take us through February, March and April when weather conditions outdoors are rarely conducive to the enjoyment of little treasures. Massed together they will open and respond to the warmth indoors. A small version on a saucer or soup plate would make a welcome gift to an elderly or sick person, especially with the added pleasure of something fragrant.

My great aunt used to make these 'islands' as she called them and they were a source of wonderment to me as a little boy. They are the first attempts at flower arranging that register in my memory. She was inventive, getting the maximum effect from the minimum of plant material, each flower shown to advantage against the moss and stones. The simplest daisies, celandines, catkins of hazel, and primroses were more precious to her than any exotic hot-house orchid might have been. She also wrote poetry and I suspect that this and the little islands made from gleanings picked on our walks together were a kind of refuge for her imagination. Many find comfort, tranquillity and peace in the creation and contemplation of loveliness, especially at times when the outer world seems inhospitable and uncaring. If flowers are earth's laughter then none can be more cheerful than these offerings of spring.

Certain leaves help to supplement our winter diet of evergreen or preserved foliage by appearing when we least expect them. Such is the case with *Arum italicum* 'Pictum', a plant similar in leaf shape to our wild Lords-and-Ladies, or Cuckoo-Pint, of woodlands and hedgerows. However, this handsome arum should not be confused with *Arum maculatum*, for it is superior in every way and of garden origin. The arrowhead-shaped leaves appear from tightly furled buds in November or December, and, depending on the weather, continue to strengthen in structure and increase in size well into spring. Each leaf is beautifully marbled and veined with grey-green over a shining, dark background, with a distinctive margin of plain green. They are narrower than those of the wild arum, with strongly reversed back lobes on one-foot stems. The flowers appear in June with a single, pale green spathe, papery in texture, sometimes mauvish, and surrounding the club-like creamy spadix. They are short-lived and once pollinated wither away to surprise us later by reappearing as fat clusters of shining green fruit on stiff stems.

Figure 4

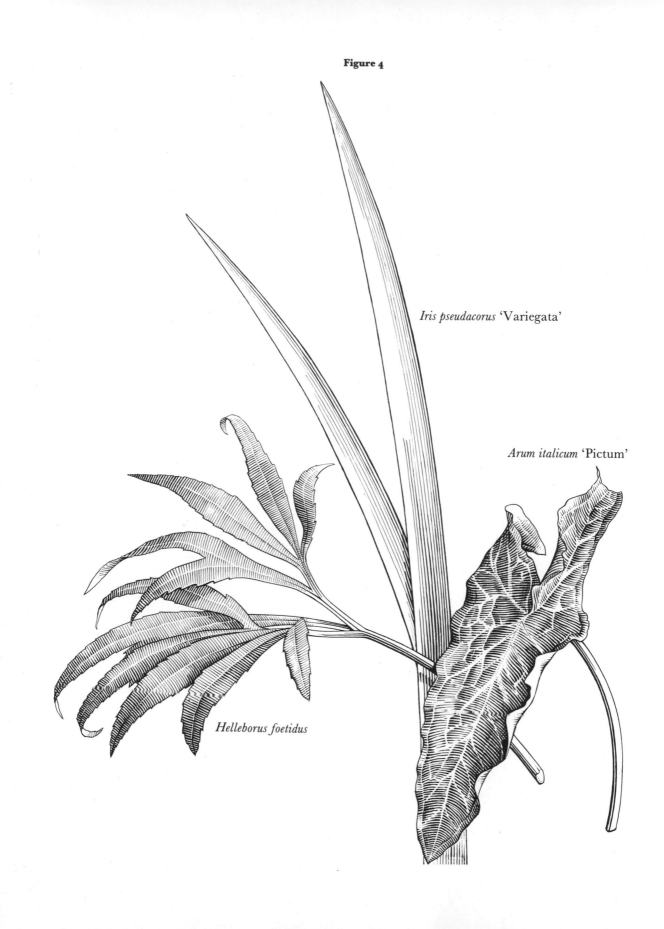

Iris pseudacorus 'Variegata'

Arum italicum 'Pictum'

Helleborus foetidus

These ripen to orange and scarlet and although probably poisonous they look luscious in autumn arrangements of fruits. The leaves are a valuable foil for the stiffness of daffodils or tulips in an arrangement. They last well if picked when mature, provided they are given a long drink in deep water. The stem ends may be gently bound with a strand of wool to discourage them from splitting under water. By midsummer the whole plant, but for the fruits, collapses and dies away ready for a period of dormancy. Planted in a woodland setting of open shade, it enjoys a cool root run in soil retentive of moisture, looking well associated with evergreen ferns and hellebores. It is because of this latter association that it is included in Figure 4 where its sagittate form contrasts well with more divided shapes.

What a fashionable family the hellebores have become, almost as lionized as the hostas, but hardly as useful for cutting. There is a certain fascination about green flowers, especially if they are accompanied by good foliage and appear at a lean time of year. I must confess I have fallen under their spell, but have become slowly disenchanted with them as cut flowers because of their propensity to wilt. Elaborate preparation to avoid this is recommended by all authorities on how to condition these temperamental beauties, but still they fail if the temperature of the room anywhere approximates to a warmth reasonable for human comfort. The Lenten hellebores are the chief offenders in this case of difficult conditioning, but their beauty is of a most desirable excellence. *Helleborus orientalis* blooms from February to April and there are many selected forms with flowers ranging from dusky purple and subtle pinks to creamy green and speckled white. The cut flowers must be mature when picked, the stems scored their entire length from flower to cut end with a penknife point. The stem ends are then boiled, their flowers protected from steam, and then finally immersed in deep, tepid water. They may still wilt and cannot abide water-retaining foams.

The most successful arrangement of Lenten hellebores I ever saw was in one of those baronial Scottish houses where the temperature necessitates as many layers of wool as can be conveniently worn without giving the impression of a walking cocoon. When I enquired of my hostess how she managed to keep the flowers fresh she shot me a furtive look and said in an undertone, 'Don't tell my husband, but they are in gin.' Somewhat baffled, I asked if her husband was a strict teetotaller, whereupon she retorted 'Oh no, but he is in whisky and wouldn't approve.' It is true that alcohol will revive most things, even if only temporarily. I have tried a weak solution of gin and water for my hellebores and it didn't seem to harm them. The correct time to pick them is when they have set seed and the stamens have fallen away. By this time the seed box is swelling and the disc of petaloid sepals will have darkened in colour.

The Corsican hellebore has suffered several name changes over the last decade and I believe we are now back almost to square one with *Helleborus lividus* subsp. *corsicus*. This evergreen sprawls about with stems of glaucous, trifoliate foliage, each leaflet having an attractive spiny edge. It starts to flower in January in shady, sheltered spots. The terminal clusters of pendant buds open to soft green, the colour of pistachio kernels. Like the hydrangea and clematis they possess petals which are modified bracts or sepals respectively and can stand being immersed in warm water to revive wilted specimens. An added attraction to the flower is the pale green nectaries at the base of each petal. Short sprays last well, but whole stems must be split, boiled and soaked.

By far the most attractive in leaf, and it is leaves which we are chiefly considering, is our native stinking hellebore. The leaves of *Helleborus foetidus* are almost black-green, a colour of masculine quality described by interior decorators as Napoleonic green. They are finely divided into nine pointed leaflets, each exquisitely fashioned with a serrated edge arranged in a semi-circle on a sturdy stalk. Picked in winter or spring, they last a long time and add a note of sombre dignity to a foliage group or as a foil to fragile flowers of *Iris stylosa*, or species crocus. An illustration of this lovely leaf appears in Figure 4. The flowers are borne in clusters in February and last in beauty three months. Smaller than the Corsican hellebores, on a branching inflorescence, each green bell is edged with maroon. Grow it in a position of semi-shade. The rosettes of new growth will break from the base giving pleasure all year, even before they burst into flower, after which they set seed and die away.

Strongly contrasting in form comes the Yellow Flag iris to complete the trio. This is chiefly a spring subject appearing from dormant rhizomes about mid-April. *Iris pseudacorus* 'Variegata' is a flower arranger's 'must', giving to an arrangement an air of distinction with its sword-like leaves of bright primrose yellow and lime green in vertical stripes. I first saw it in an uncle's garden when I was about ten years old and it soon found a place in my little garden to contrast with *Hosta fortunei* 'Albopicta' in form and to relate to it in colour. I was, therefore, rather disappointed when by midsummer the whole quiver of leaves turned mid-green. After thirty years I have learnt to expect this change and I appreciate the plant all the more for the months it is at its best. The leaf tips are brightest when it first appears by the waterside; by mid-May the variegation is reflected in a tranquil pool which doubles its effectiveness. The yellow flowers veined with brown are of little cutting value and I would recommend their removal from newly established plants, because once these set seed the variegation disappears. If left, the green seed pods burst in September, to display light brown seeds. Cut material is easy to condition requiring only shallow water: in deep water the heart of the leaf-spray becomes slimy and rots. This plant will survive in sun or shade, but does best by water and in water where it forms a useful transition from bank to pond.

Tulips must be among the most trying of spring flowers to arrange because of their habit of continuing to grow after being cut. Once this fact has been accepted we can go ahead and enjoy their beauty expressed in such a diversity of forms and colours. I must confess I have little use for the forced florist's tulips, because these are so lacking in strength after a few days in water and are absolutely maddening in a formal design, be it mass or line. The garden varieties, picked when young, can be relied upon to behave better without the drunken stance of their over-drawn predecessors. There can be few flowers with greater poise and elegance, their chalice-like form set off by stems of appropriate strength. The way to arrange them is openly and lightly, so that they have room to assume candelabra-style curves without interfering too much with the pattern of other companions. My favourites include the lily-flowered, peony-flowered and viridiflora tulips. There are many others, all excellent for cutting or as garden decorators, but these three are the flower arranger's choice.

Plate IV shows lily-flowered tulips 'Mariette' used with other spring subjects in such a way that the flowers can continue to develop without detriment to the design. The idea of two matching containers unified by a carved wooden base helps to create asymmetric balance. The tall vase is modern Chinese with a calligraphic design and celadon glaze. The lower rectangle is of my own design and of the same soft colouring. Branches of budding apple blossom form the outline, with a simplicity borrowed from the Orient. The focal area is formed by three gorgeous blooms of *Paeonia suffruticosa* 'Souvenir de la Reine Elizabete', this rather cumbersome name often being abbreviated to 'Elizabeth'. The fully double flowers open in early May, and in one disastrous season my peony bore over thirty buds – a feat never again attempted – all but two of which were killed by a late frost. It usually contents itself with around sixteen blooms of carmine rose with a touch of purple at the base of each petal. The foliage of this tree peony is of a glaucous grey-green and prompted the choice of a container with Chinese affinities. Young leaves of *Hosta sieboldiana elegans* help to consolidate the design, their glaucous bloom still intact, while acting as a transitional movement between the two containers are the pendant necklaces of *Dicentra spectabilis*. This flower has many colloquial names including Bleeding Heart, Lady-in-the-Bath and Lady's Locket. It is a plant of great elegance, with a fragility of appearance which quite belies its underlying toughness. The flowers and ferny, grey-green leaves appear in April and continue in great beauty for six weeks, constantly dividing and developing more flowers from branching side shoots. It can easily be forced in a cold greenhouse and is often used this way for municipal conservatory decorations. A cool, moist place suits it best with some shelter from cold winds or frost, which might cut its precocious perennial appearance.

The design has an openness which enables us to enjoy the circular window in a setting with a white and crimson-red colour-scheme. The mechanical support consists of a rectangular pinholder in the lower bowl and wire netting in the upright vase. By using containers at split levels more emphasis can be given to the inter-connecting space. This example stresses the importance of not using too many materials.

Three foliage plants illustrated in Figure 5 come into the cossetted category, but I make no excuse for their inclusion. All demand a sheltered, woodland position with a moist, acid soil, rich in leaf-mould. The first is an evergreen groundcover called *Galax aphylla*. Anyone who has American flower arrangement books of the fifties will be familiar with leaves contrived into flowers like camellias, but these are not for me. I was delighted to use this leaf from the Smokey Mountains at Colonial Williamsburg, Virginia, not far from its natural habitat. It is widely sold in the United States as cut foliage and a tougher, more attractive, little leaf would be hard to find. Of rounded shape up to five inches across it is shiny green, beautifully veined. The whole clump will acquire a coppery burnished tint in winter and last for six weeks or more as cut material on short, wiry stems. The name Fairies' Wand refers to the dainty, white flowers which

appear at midsummer. It is a pity it is not more widely known and grown in Britain.

The Mahonia family supplies us with some of our most useful shrubs for cutting and probably the most widely grown and picked is *Mahonia japonica*. This handsome shrub is a great feature in our garden, forming a thicket twelve feet long and over six feet high. The leaves are pinnate, divided into at least six to eight pairs of leaflets and arranged in handsome whorls over a foot across. The flowers appear in November, continuing spasmodically till February. Their fragrance, redolent of Lilies-of-the-Valley, will fill a room. Not a long-lasting cut flower, it is better if the entire truss can be spared and the woody stems crushed. The evergreen leaves have many uses both fresh and glycerined, even used reversed. There are still nurserymen who sell *Mahonia bealii* as *Mahonia japonica*, but this is not the same plant, not nearly so big and showy or with such long, lax flower trusses. *Mahonia lomariifolia* is not for the average garden, being much too tender with leaves of up to twenty pairs of spiny leaflets, resembling a dover sole picked clean to the bone. A cross between *Mahonia japonica* and *Mahonia lomariifolia* has given us *Mahonia* 'Charity', which is in many ways a flower arranger's plant. Unfortunately the flowers are not very fragrant, but the formation of the leaves compensates for this defect. They are most graceful, of an indestructible quality as cut material, and worth waiting for. The shrub is slow to settle down, but will eventually branch out and form a dramatic feature.

I have tried and failed in the past with the exquisite *Pieris formosa forrestii*, the Flame-of-the-Forest bush, but at long last a plant of the 'Wakehurst' form, purchased from Bodnant, has established itself. It cannot stand cold, biting winds in early spring when the leaf buds are most vulnerable. Much as I dislike winter-bandaged plants, some extra protection is often necessary. The effort is well worthwhile for the plants put forth brilliant shrimp-pink and red rosettes of shining foliage as spring advances.

Figure 5

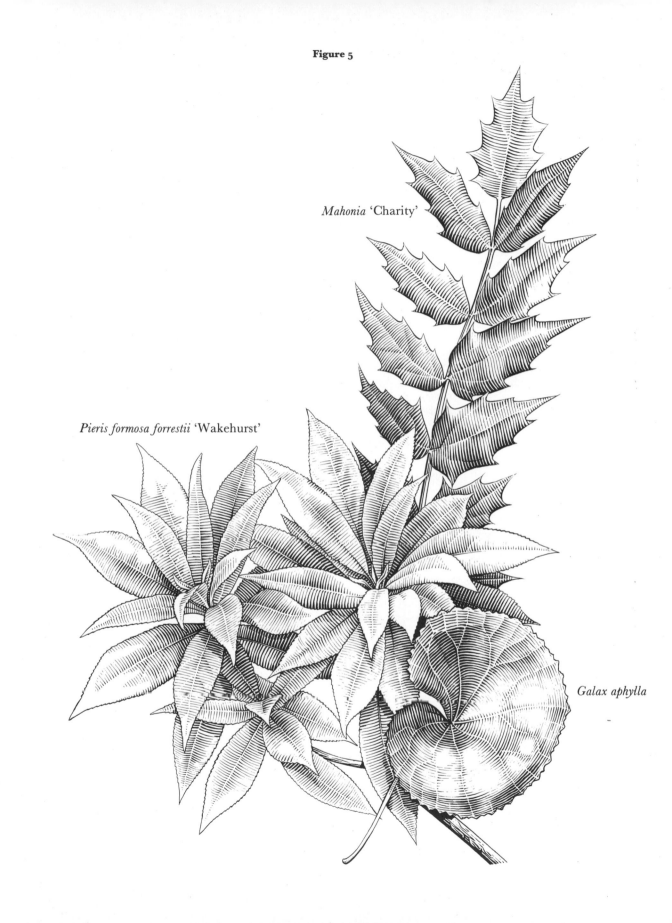

Mahonia 'Charity'

Pieris formosa forrestii 'Wakehurst'

Galax aphylla

Short pieces cut from the established plants of friends have proved to be long-lasting and always create a *succès fou* at a demonstration.

Strong winds are one of the most limiting factors in gardening, but soil conditions also have great bearing on what we can or cannot grow. All three plants in Figure 5 need acid soil, that is to say they are calcifuge or lime-hating. Knowing what type of soil you have is essential for good cultivation. Acid to neutral soils offer greater scope to the gardener than do alkaline conditions. Unfortunately we mostly have to accept what we have in our particular area. I feel it is a complete waste of time to struggle to grow such lime-hating plants as rhododendrons, camellias, ericas, kalmias, etc., if you do not have the acidity and high rainfall they require. Gardening in chalk or, worse still, light sandy soil can be almost as frustrating as really solid clay. Try to study what flourishes in your neighbourhood, in gardens with similar soil conditions and then select the best forms of the plants that grow well. This will be far more rewarding in the long run than constantly struggling with the wrong type of plants for your soil pH.

It is most necessary to feed the soil, for all plants require food and soil must be constantly enriched to encourage healthy, disease free growth. Poor, dry, impoverished soils lacking in humus will never produce the lush growth which enables us to pick from plants for our decorations. To keep the soil in good health it must have a constant supply of decomposed organic matter. Stable or farmyard manure can be a costly if not unobtainable commodity for town and city dwellers. Home composted refuse offers a substitute and no garden should be without its compost heap. Leaf mould and peat can rarely be gathered in the wild, but where this is possible it repays the effort involved. Mulches of lawn mowings, spent hops, wood chippings, processed sewage and other substitutes all play their role in helping to conserve moisture around plants, although their actual nutritional content may not be high.

III Dish garden for a guest room
IV Line design with peonies

3 Early Summer

Early summer in Britain, from mid-May into June, is a special period, when the likelihood of frost is past. Increasing warmth and long daylight hours accelerate development and each day marks the unfolding of some special treasure or long anticipated friend. It is a time of intense activity, for so much rapid growth creates a myriad jobs to be done. Staking, tying, hoeing, planting, watering, weeding, feeding, mulching, mowing, edging absorb our every available moment. But through it all comes the realization that the promises of spring are fast becoming the reality of summer.

This season brings the greatest variety of flowers for picking with the emphasis chiefly on pastel colours. The foliage of deciduous trees and shrubs has an unsurpassable vigour and brilliance. With such an enormous variety of plants for possible inclusion in this chapter, it is extremely difficult to discriminate. The emphasis is again on foliage which will furnish the garden for the next six months, supplying the arranger with forms, colours and textures of unrivalled beauty and diversity.

We will begin by considering three plants, illustrated in Figure 6, useful for their neutrality of colour yet endued with interesting surface textures. The first is a tree, and the only tree I have included in the line illustrations. Whitebeam is a familiar sight on limestone soils in the south of England, but the form *Sorbus aria* 'Lutescens' is much more arresting. The newly opening buds of this medium-sized tree resemble pale, celadon-green magnolias poised on black branches. The upper and lower surfaces of the soft, felted leaves are covered with a fine meal or farinose dust which imparts to the whole tree a strange luminosity. Seen side-lit, against the darkening sky of a sudden storm, the effect is quite electrifying, the upturned leaves shimmering with light. By late May the leaves are fully expanded making long, sweeping sprays useful for pedestals or other large designs. The young foliage preserves well in a glycerine and water solution, changing to pale buff but retaining the tomentose texture. Repeated rain may diminish this effect in the garden, but reversed branches will still display this attractive feature. I have an especially small-leaved form among my half-dozen trees and this can be seen used in Plate VI.

The next foliage plant is really a tree, but is best treated as a pollarded bush – in this guise *Eucalyptus perriniana* develops a constant supply of juvenile shoots bearing disc-like leaves threaded along wiry stalks. The effect is silvery-grey with a pewtery bloom. Its hardiness is questionable, but a sheltered corner and winter protection in the first years are worth the effort. For more exposed sites *Eucalyptus gunnii* would be a safer if less eye-catching choice. Sprays of this gum last a long time in water and preserve in glycerine without the over-powering smell which attends the commercial product made from it and reminds me of the school sick-room. Constant cutting will ensure a supply of new shoots and keep the plant within bounds.

Why include *Senecio laxifolius*, you may ask, when it is so commonplace? But how useful it is. This New Zealander is a boon for coastal gardeners, but is equally at home inland and forms our staple diet for year-round grey foliage. Perhaps if it were difficult to grow it would be more valued. Few shrubs are so accommodating, keeping up a supply of curving sprays of oval, grey-green leaves edged with white, which repeats the underside and stem colour. It is easily trained up a wall or will make low, hummocky bushes. Short side shoots taken with a heel root easily, so a stock of young plants is always on hand. The bright yellow daisies are of little decorative value and I prefer to remove them rather than let the plant be weakened. Considerable confusion exists about the name: it is frequently referred to as *Senecio greyii*. Both plants have obscure origins in the wild state, therefore it might be safer to call it by the newly proposed name of *Senecio* (Dunedin Hybrid) 'Sunshine'.

The decoration in Plate V exemplifies the traditional mass-style of flower arrangement on a grand scale. The container sited on a seventeenth-century oak chest is a large, copper fish kettle. Copper utensils are a good choice, for they usually hold ample water and have fungicidal properties, working in the same way as a copper coin helps to keep flower water fresh. The flowers are elevated in a series of plastic cones of graduated size, firmly lashed to a garden cane with insulating tape. The cane is in turn impaled on a heavy pinholder, after passing down through several layers of two-inch mesh wire netting. The cut ends of the netting are firmly anchored to the handles of the container. Absolute firmness and rigidity are essential before the construction of a large group, attention to firm mechanics being worth all the initial effort involved.

The setting of the entrance hall allows scope for a decoration of above average proportions, to be viewed from three sides. A portrait of 1710 with gilded Carolean frame balances the asymmetrical placement of the design at one end of the chest. The boy's gold cloak picks up the flower colours with its diagonal movement.

The lime-green outline material is of *Acer negundo* 'Aureo-marginatum', which, grown as a shrub, is at its most striking in spring and early summer. The divided leaves of pale lime green are bordered with cream variegation, an effect carried all summer. Long, curving leaves of cardoon, described in Chapter 4, were first hardened in boiling water for one minute. The whole colour-scheme places emphasis on a mixture of paler tints of green, pink, gold, apricot and yellow. The tallest placements of *Iris germanica* 'Edward of Windsor' act as the pivot of such a mixed colour-scheme. This aristocrat has delicate, apricot-pink standard petals, with falls of the same tint overlaid with a fine stencilling of

lilac-grey, the orange stamen adding a highlight at the junction of the two. This unusual colour is the catalyst for the fusion of antirrhinums, azaleas and spray chrysanthemums in deeper tones. The pale pink of *Rhododendron* 'Mrs Anthony Waterer', with its distinctive green marking on the upper petal, has been further accentuated by the entire defoliation of each spray. The removal of heavy, shabby leaves always helps to lighten the effect of this genus in a decoration, except of course in those species where the foliage is of special merit.

The focal area is dominated by two tree peonies, *Paeonia suffruticosa* 'Chromatella', cut at the half-open stage. Each bloom is a mass of crumpled, silky, yellow petals finely edged with bronze, and gives off a delicious scent like ripe peaches. I can't think of any flower more lovely or more temperamental to condition, for unless the flower is almost floating on water it will wilt. To ensure this requirement, the short stems were arranged in individually wide cones of water concealed amidst the foliage. In this way they lasted several days. As the flower of this variety is top-heavy on weak stems, it always disappears from sight under its leaves in the garden, so this seems a good way to enjoy such perfection at close quarters.

Rhododendron 'Tortoise-shell Champagne' is for me in a class apart shared only by 'Unique' and 'Idealist', all three varieties of great distinction. The colour of the first is an exact match to the iris. Rather late-blooming, it will appeal to the discerning, and appears on the top right and left side of the arrangement. The pendant flower heads of *Allium siculum*, discussed in Chapter 7, are a strange combination of waxy green and apricot with a maroon centre. Shell-pink gerbera daisies add wide-eyed freshness, and the whole design is pulled together by the bold, glaucous blue leaves of *Hosta sieboldiana elegans*. Towards the top of the picture the striped acid green and lime of *Iris pseudacorus* 'Variegata' helps to foil the bare stems of the iris flowers and conceal the tubes used for elevation. This plant is described in Chapter 2. A criticism levelled against the

Figure 6

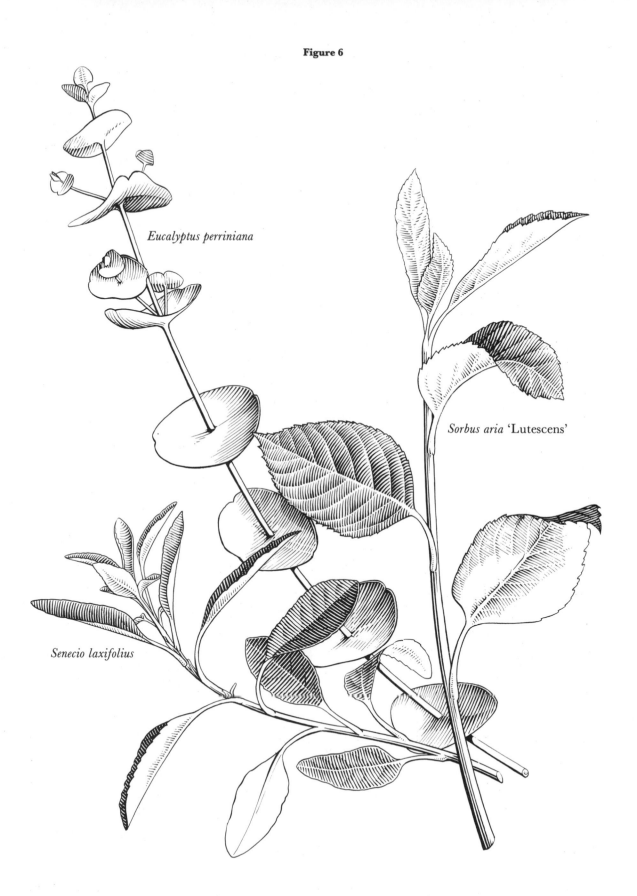

Eucalyptus perriniana

Sorbus aria 'Lutescens'

Senecio laxifolius

bearded iris as a cut flower is that it does not last long in water. This is true of the individual flowers, but if cut when the top bud is opening, the side and subsidiary buds will continue to develop. This is partly why they were placed at the top of the design, another reason being that their three-dimensional form should be enjoyed from all angles. Faded flowers can be nipped away, enabling new buds to open. Such a design requires room and a plain background to set it off, but it could easily be reduced to a smaller domestic scale.

Many of our early summer flower arrangements rely on the beauty of deciduous shrubs for outline material and there are a great many worth having in the garden for this dual purpose. The hardest part is deciding which ranks as being especially useful with so many clamouring for inclusion. The three shrubs in Figure 7 have yellow-green in common as their predominant colouring. The intensity of this will largely be influenced by where you grow them. A yellow-leaved shrub will usually develop brighter, brassier colouring the stronger the sunlight, whereas the same plant grown in deep shade may appear almost mid-green, so site is important for all three.

The first is an all-the-year-rounder and found its way in here simply because of its colouring. We all know what a rapid growing hedge *Lonicera nitida* can make, so the variety 'Baggeson's Gold' can be expected to do the same. It is in fact rather slow, but once established becomes a thick, impenetrable tangle of fine, woody shoots. I have three growing as a group and they occupy a space some fifteen feet across and six feet high. They grew eight years ago in a shady border, rather dejected-looking specimens with no hint of the yellow and pink tints that an open, sunny site will produce. It was with some trepidation that I removed an enormous topiarized clump of the plain green, growing in a large island bed, and replaced it with the three of free-standing, anaemic-looking, golden form. The result is a magnificent unclipped clump, foiled for contrast by a large

bush of *Berberis thunbergii* 'Atropurpurea Superba' and the delicate-leaved beauty of *Robinia pseudoacacia* 'Frisia', so beloved by Beverley Nichols, grown as a feathered half-standard.

The golden lonicera provides the decorator with long-lasting, dainty sprays of foliage, possibly at their best by August, when the long, new shoots of small, oval leaves are tinged with pink on wiry maroon stems, the individual leaflets almost ivory-coloured. The alternate and opposite arrangement of the side twigs gives it an openness and poise useful for lightening an arrangement. Short, curving, single sprays provide material for dainty arrangements, so do not be put off by my description of mammoth plantings – one bush will be found to earn its keep.

Rather more fragile and of a deciduous nature is the golden-leaved form of Mock Orange. I have two favourites amongst the *Philadelphus* family, the first described in Chapter 5; the second here and illustrated in Figure 7. *Philadelphus coronarius* 'Aureus' grows about six feet tall and I now realize mine was planted too close to the edge of the border. However, it is only some four feet at present. The spring leaves appear in April and by May are the most vivid chartreuse yellow, especially in full sun. In a very exposed position, brown scorched patches develop, spoiling the overall appearance. The oval, serrated leaves are thin-textured but light up the garden, and as cut material there is the added attraction of sweetly scented flowers reminiscent of cottage gardens. Unfortunately, it is not an elegant grower like *Philadelphus* 'Beauclerk' which simply cannot put a twig wrong. The best sprays are the long, new shoots which develop from judicious pruning of the older, twiggy growth. It is a temptation to pick these pieces all the time, resulting in a rather squat, clipped bush. Try to thin as you pick with an eye to the overall shape of the bush, as well as taking that coveted piece to cascade out of your vase. By mid-July the brightest colour effect has dimmed and the bush returns to a more uniform green, able to get on with

Figure 7

Lonicera nitida 'Baggesen's Gold'

Physocarpus opulifolius 'Luteus'

Philadelphus coronarius 'Aureus'

growing unthreatened by our depredation.

Another shrub which behaves in a very similar way to the Mock Orange is the more robust *Physocarpus opulifolius* 'Luteus'. As its name implies, it is more yellow than green. Not regarded as a connoisseur's plant, it makes rapid growth, providing long, arching wands lime yellow in spring and early summer. These are at their best when newly expanding and last better at this stage than when fully open. They add a highlight to any decoration and associate well with long-stemmed, lily-flowered tulips, especially the dark red varieties. Boil and crush the woody stem ends and soak overnight, but do not immerse. Material I used at a demonstration, and later found wilted, quickly revived when placed in shallow, hot water. Avoid damaging young or tender foliage with steam by wrapping all but the stem ends in waxed paper. By midsummer the shrub has flowered and the large, currant-shaped leaves are coarse and uninteresting, but already it is making the rapid growth which will furnish us with pedestal-sized sprays for next spring. Like the philadelphus it should be sited with a dark background and in a sunny but not over-exposed position to avoid leaf scorch. Pruning is bound to happen when you pick, but some tall leader shoots must be left to form the future framework of the bush. Old flowered wood can be removed after the spiraea-like white flowers have faded, clearing weak twiggery to open up the centre. The leaves assume a bronze hue in autumn, so it earns a place on that count too.

This is a season of rapid change and what is at its best one moment is gone in a few days' time, especially if a sudden heat wave accelerates the process. The new growth is soft and requires more attention to conditioning than at any other season. The pedestal in the dining-room (see Plate VI) is of an ideal scale for an average-sized room; it measures four feet high, with a tripod foot of sturdy carved pine eighteen inches wide. It has sentimental value for me because it was my first purchase as a student gardener over twenty years ago when £7 10s (£7.50) seemed a

lot of money. How values have changed and what pleasure I have had from that initial investment. A flat pewter plate supports a circular baking-tin and an assemblage of cones all made to appear as if they grow naturally from the cornucopia of flowers held by the cherub. Being of wood, the pedestal is heavy and has great stability, but when using a more flimsy, wrought iron one be sure that one of the three feet is facing forward and two behind as there is less likelihood of its tipping forwards used this way. I prefer to use a *torchère* or column which has some substance about it as this helps to balance the width of the composition, thus avoiding the appearance of a coloured lollipop on a stick. The whole essence of this pedestal style is the opportunity it affords to curve downwards, below the horizontal line drawn through the focal point. When selecting materials the choice of graceful, curving sprays of blossom or foliage becomes of primary importance. Try to avoid straight, stiff stems such as gladioli, grown with a regimental precision, for these will only stick out at rigid angles and look awkward and unnatural. The argument that flower arrangement is unnatural anyway can be sometimes heard from gardeners, but what could be more artificial than a garden with so many plants under control as opposed to nature's wildness? The secret is to make the effect in both appear natural, for this surely is the art which conceals art.

The key to the colour-scheme in Plate VI is the Persian carpet of many pastel pinks, blues and mauves, and early June abounds with these colours. The outline material consists of reversed sprays of sorbus, the small-leaved version already mentioned. *Ceanothus x* veitchianus is not a likely subject for picking, but seemed such a perfect colour I decided to risk it. Though some cut and transported to a lecture proved a failure, the newly expanding buds shown here lasted three days – an example of catching a plant just at its moment of perfection which can never be recaptured for that year. How brief are our lives when measured by such an annual fleeting moment! Fortunately, there is always something coming to perfection to help fulfil our hopes and dreams.

The clematis must be one of the most useful and varied of genera for the floral artist, the large-flowered hybrids being the most showy for pedestal designs. *Clematis lanuginosa* 'Nellie Moser' is used here together with forced hydrangea cut from a pot plant to create the centre of the design. They are both false flowers in that the petals are really petaloid sepals or bracts and have a stronger texture than true petals. This botanical fact helps us to know that we can immerse the heads of both flowers to condition them. This is certainly good for the hydrangea, which was already mature, having previously given six weeks' pleasure as a pot plant. Remove all the leaves as these take too much moisture from the flower head, as well as clashing with the colour-scheme. Crush the stems and immerse for two or three hours, shaking off surplus moisture before arranging. The clematis are picked with about six inches of stem, which should be lightly crushed, and the flowers are then floated on water. There is a certain stage when they will hold, half-way between the opening bud and the fully mature flower: catching this requires some experimentation. These flowers lasted four days in the pedestal and were later used at a demonstration, in a heat wave two days after, still in perfect condition. The secret lies in the pre-conditioning and hardening of the flowers in a cool place. One trick I always resort to with them in a large group is to arrange them in single glass tubes of water, taped to slender canes. These are carefully concealed amidst the foliage and other flowers. Other more accommodating flowers consist of *Rhododendron* 'Sappho', defoliated for lightness, and the mauve heads of *Allium aflatunense*. What useful flowers these decorative onions are, growing in graduated sizes from self-sown bulbs and lasting a long time in water. Any odour of onion is only perceptible at the moment of recutting the stem ends. Other flowers used in the pedestal include florist's carnations 'Orchid

Beauty', double stocks, *Iris sibirica* and long-spurred hybrid aquilegias. These perennial columbines were grown from seed and have bicoloured flowers in unusual combinations. The dainty foliage, often assuming mauvish tones in dry weather, is also attractive in its grey-green state. The after-care of the decoration consists of a daily topping up of all the tubes, cones and Oasis foundation. It is also beneficial to syringe with a fine mist of vapour over the whole design, having first taken precautions to protect surrounding furnishings. One imposing decoration in a room is always more effective than several smaller ones. Placed diagonally across from the main entrance it creates an arresting line of vision. This pedestal usually stands in the right angle of two walls which allows for a much more open style of design without the necessity to fill in the sides and back, as in the entrance-hall arrangement.

The hostas must be amongst the best known and most cherished of foliage plants for the flower arranger, supplying lanceolate-oval or heart-shaped leaves, many with beautiful variegation and of a sculptured quality which makes them a joy to pick and a useful adjunct to any garden. Like so many plants of Japanese origin they require cool growing conditions – preferably some shade and a constant moisture supply. They are a feature of the garden at Heslington where fifteen different species and varieties are growing. Their general ease of culture, propagation being by division during the dormant season, ensures that they can be relied upon to give years of useful service. My first clump was 'collected' from the vicarage compost heap, surreptitiously removed through a gap in the hedge, my eye caught by its lime-yellow colouring and my hand compounded to the felony by the desire for possession. I was eight years old. Few plants have served me better, especially in early summer when *Hosta fortunei* 'Albopicta' is at its most brilliant, lime yellow with a green edge, lime green where the two overlap. That clump, like the talent of silver well used, has been increased thirty-fold. In its wake have come many more distinctive forms, added to whenever possible. Their names are a horrifying jumble with many synonyms to add to the confusion. I bow to Mr Graham Thomas's superior nomenclatural knowledge for my direction rather than be caught on the shifting sands of general usage. *Hosta fortunei* 'Albopicta' may be a good start, especially in the unlikely event that you are eight years old, but it does have the disadvantage of going all green later in the season. This happens immediately the weather turns hot and sunny, usually by mid-June. From then onwards it is a nondescript affair, with washy mauve flowers. Others command our attention, the most useful being *Hosta sieboldiana elegans* of architectural proportions, each leaf measuring as much as twelve inches long by the same across. The newly emerging purple-tipped shoots resemble asparagus and are about as succulent to slugs. For some mysterious reason we are not troubled by these pests in any quantity and I am sure this is because of Norman Puckering's scrupulous tidiness in these moist, shady areas where they breed. Poisonous pellets and after-dark trapping safaris help to keep them under control.

One of the most useful hostas for small arrangements is *Hosta undulata undulata* illustrated in Figure 8. This is one of the neatest with lanceolate leaves of creamy white narrowly edged with mid-green and with a distinct spiral twist towards the pointed leaf tip. The leaves last up to three weeks in water and are a delightful foil for small flowers. The flower spike is also bone white with mauve trumpets dispersed at irregular intervals along its twelve-inch length. For the front of the border it must have shade as the leaves will scorch in strong sunshine.

A little larger and very similar in leaf but with more green is *Hosta undulata univittata*, sent to me as a substitute for something else I ordered at the Chelsea Show. It started life with this handicap, but now, several clumps later, is proving its worth about the garden, standing up to more open conditions.

Much more to my taste is *Hosta ventricosa*

'Variegata', an outstanding sport with green, wavy, heart-shaped leaves deeply veined and edged with cream. The overlapping of cream on to green creates further shadings. The finely pointed tip of the leaf is distinguished by a sensuous curve.

Many flower arrangers are drawn to the curious flowers of the astrantias, but whilst appreciating fully their quaint form and muted colouring, I do not like their smell. The redeeming feature of *Astrantia major* 'Sunningdale Variegated', introduced in 1966, is its foliage. The deeply divided, five-lobed leaves have a serrated edge and are borne singly on long stems. They are generously splashed and marbled with creamy white on green, later changing to cream and yellow. Two young leaves appear in the decoration in Plate III. Whilst most of the green species, native of upland Alpine meadows, appreciate some shade and moisture, this plant needs more sunshine. A drawing of it appears in Figure 8. I prefer to remove the flower umbels, as this helps to keep up the supply of leaves, for there are others with better flowers. Cut material lasts well after an initial long, cool drink in deep water.

Mrs Fish did much to popularize these Masterworts with their flowers like a Victorian pincushion, the tiny florets backed by a collar of pointed bracts called the involucre, giving it a star-like effect. The size and length of these varies in each species and some of the forms of garden origin, known as 'Shaggy', are now finding more specific clonal names as a result of the efforts of Mr Jim Archibald. *Astrantia carniolica* 'Rubra' is a smaller plant in all parts with umbels of deep dirty crimson flowers, destined to send arrangers into ecstasies – but keep it for the flower exhibition rather than the bedside posy!

As May gives way to June the herbaceous peonies are at their best. This aristocratic family contains many plants of superlative garden value not only for their flowers but also for foliage and seed pods. Unfortunately the flowers of the single species do not last long and

Figure 8

Astrantia major 'Sunningdale Variegated'

Hosta undulata undulata

Hosta ventricosa 'Variegata'

are easily damaged by bad weather. Transient beauty of this calibre is made all the more precious by its ephemerality. In this special category comes a Caucasian princess with a tongue twister of a name. *Paeonia mlokosewitschii* has primrose-yellow flowers held on two-foot stems over leaves of softest grey-green, tinged at first with bronze. The unfolding flower reveals a boss of golden stamens clustered around the pinky-red stigma. The effect is ravishing. Mine seed themselves from pods of unexpected brilliance, with cherry-red and indigo-blue seeds. Another single is *Paeonia wittmanniana* with a hybrid called 'Le Printemps', a fleeting beauty in an elusive tint of pale creamy-buff flushed with pink, set off by bronze foliage. Both bloom in early May.

The Asiatic *Paeonia lactiflora* 'Whitleyi Major' has large, white, very fragrant flowers, the single petals filled out with golden stamens around a pink stigma. From this species the Chinese bred many hybrids, the forerunners of more modern varieties. These fulsome doubles are heavy-headed and require staking to prevent them filling with rain and collapsing. 'Festiva Maxima' has huge, white flowers with the occasional crimson fleck. 'Sarah Bernhardt' and 'Lady Alexander Duff' are pink and lovely, like the ladies they perpetuate. Between the double and single types come those in the Imperial group. These hybrids have outer petals forming a bowl filled with slender, pointed petals or filaments: botanically these are modified stamens with a petaloid function. One of the best specimens in the group is 'Bowl of Beauty' with an outer cup of sugar-pink petals filled with creamy-white filaments, the central stigma raspberry red. Another to grow is the neat 'Queen Alexandra', white with a curly golden centre. Messrs Kelway of Langport, Somerset, have raised many varieties and specialize in this slow-growing but reliable genus.

Close on the heels of peonies come the Oriental poppies. Only three commend themselves for inclusion. Some years ago Messrs Suttons of Reading offered seed in 'art shades'; from a mixed bag of seedlings I selected a soft salmon pink and a dirty maroon. Mrs Chatto gave me 'Cedric's Pink', a seedling selected by Sir Cedric Morris. The flowers are greyish-pink, decidedly off-beat and, like that old variety 'Perry's White', look best when grown or arranged with grey foliages. As cut flowers they should be picked early in the day just as the sepal cap falls away leaving the crumpled silk of the expanding petals. The cut ends must be singed in a flame prior to a deep drink. Arranged in water they will last several days, developing to display the maroon-black blotches at the petal base matching the black stamen and seed box.

4 Roses

My first awareness of roses can be dated exactly. On my sixth birthday my family moved house and I remember it as if yesterday. Early June in the Pennine Hills is not the heady affair it may be elsewhere, but it was the time when I first discovered roses. I have only to put my nose to an apricot bloom of 'Madame Edouard Herriot' to be able to recapture that day. The garden was neat and small, set about with a rustic pergola covered with roses, which were to become to this day constant reminders of happy childhood – long, leisurely summer days when the horrors of the Second World War seemed something belonging only to the world of grown-ups. The creamy-pink perfection of 'Madame Butterfly' still has that evocative effect on me as does the fragrance of 'Dr Van Fleet'. This climbing Wichuriana hybrid grew from a seemingly inhospitable hole in the asphalt path, against a castellated brick wall by the kitchen door. It was my happy duty to dead-head it and this task I took seriously. It bore hundreds of flowers in clusters, so that once the central bloom had faded, many smaller side buds developed, each a perfect little shell-pink rose. The foliage was shiny and clear with few blemishes or greenfly to disfigure the sprays I cut with such care.

Flowers can date one and those rose varieties of the thirties are still with us, a little less vigorous, a lot less fashionable, but still loved. Thirty years later my move to Heslington brought me into contact with a garden already decked with roses in such profusion that they were breathtaking. My first visit to this house was again in early June and I little dreamt I would one day live amidst such beauty. A bowl of roses in strange mauves and pinks placed on a delicate eighteenth-century table caught my eye and gradually a new world opened, the old roses of Mrs Spry's books came to life. It wasn't until I began to know the garden thoroughly that I realized how varied and comprehensive was the collection amassed here by Nina, Lady Deramore. The credit for this must go in part to Mr Graham Stuart Thomas, the world expert on old shrub roses. Together they positioned and planted the many roses at Heslington, where the mellow brick walls of the house and out-buildings gave support to the climbers, which were painstakingly trained by Norman Puckering, the gardener. They are still a lovely sight in early June but are gradually being replaced as their constitutions weaken.

The old shrub roses are arranged in a less formal setting, with gently curving paths edged with grey and glaucous foliage plants. Many were immortalized by Pierre Joseph Redouté who painted them so perfectly between 1817 and 1824. They still evoke our Regency period and although others owe their origin to the later Victorian hybridizers, the smaller, scented French roses have greater refinement and charm. It was at La Malmaison that the Empress Josephine gathered together so many of these roses. Strange that the artist she commanded to record them on paper should be remembered long after his patroness was forgotten. To become better acquainted with these beauties one must read Mr Graham Stuart Thomas's *Old Shrub Roses.**

Plate VII shows a modern creation which attempts to capture the spirit of that age, formality and gaiety intermingled. To make such a cone is easy and a favourite way of using short-stemmed flowers when only a few of each kind can be spared.

Choose a container which is formal in shape, preferably a classical goblet style, with a foot or base heavy enough to support the visual and actual weight of the cone. The container illustrated is particularly appropriate as it is of bronze mounted on Sienese marble, with neo-classical feet and a gothic patterned tracery, which dates it exactly to the Regency Period

---

* Phoenix House, London, 1955 (reprinted 1966).

1800–30. The fine ormolu collar and lip give it an added elegance; it is one of a pair. A shallow patty-tin fits inside the rim. On to this tin is fitted a roll of one-inch mesh wire netting shaped into a slender cone. The cone is filled from the apex downwards with pieces of Oasis cut to fit, and pieces used only once or twice are adequate for the job; they must be well soaked. The special feature of this cone is the ground cover of reindeer moss. This moss is found in Northern pine forests and on the tundra of Lapland. It constitutes the basic diet of reindeer which grub it out of the snow covered wastes. Its colour, when fresh, is an exquisite soft green, like a tone from a Chinese vase. It has the properties of a sponge, softening and expanding rapidly when soaked in water or shrivelling up into a hard, grey loofah-like ball when dry. The use of this moss obviates the need to cover all the Oasis with flowers or foliage, being both economical as well as decorative. It can be used again and again and is obtainable from florists as well as gathered in the wild. Each cluster of tufts is wired into place with a soft iron rose wire of 24 gauge, six inches long. As the mossing process considerably thickens the shape of the cone it is important to anticipate this by making the wire-netting base a tight, narrow circle.

The flowers are chiefly a selection of old shrub roses starting at the top left with 'Petite de Hollande', an exquisitely formed variety of *Rosa centifolia* suitable for small gardens. A Provence rose, it is more compact in habit than many of the other varieties of *Rosa centifolia*. Like a cabbage rose in miniature, another name is 'Pompon des Dames' which suits it admirably for this fanciful decoration. Buds of the 'Common Moss' can be seen at the top right, their mossy stems and calyces looking like something from a Victorian valentine. The central roses are from the Bourbon group and, therefore, not strictly contemporary with the vase. However, they are gorgeous in their perfume and abundance, my favourite being 'Madame Lauriol de Barny' raised in 1868, seen in the centre of the picture. It has silvery-pink flowers in such profusion as to

weigh the bush down to the ground when in full bloom. Unfortunately, it only flowers once in the year, in mid-June. To the right of centre is 'Commandant Beaurepaire', a spectacular striped rose with tones of carmine pink, rose madder and purple. The lowest blooms on the right are of another moss rose, 'Louis Grimard'. The characteristic buds, heavily mossed, open to reveal rich, flat blooms with muddled centres and rolled petals of a lilac-cerise colour, all quite distinctive in shape.

Other flowers include clematis 'Comtesse de Bouchaud', the soft mauve-pink colouring exactly matching the paler bed draperies. Small sprays of the purple 'Violette', a rambler introduced in 1921 and the only 'modern' rose included in this selection, are used centrally beside the clematis. Single florets of pale blue delphinium and deeper blue lateral sprays add contrast. The curious pincushion flowers of Masterwort echo the pink of the clematis and the grey-green of the moss. These strange flowers emit a rather stale odour, but this particular *Astrantia maxima* seems free of this fault. Spikes of lavender and trembling clusters of Quaking Grass, *Briza maxima*, all add lightness to the outline and the slightest suggestion of movement to an otherwise static shape. Blue-grey, thick-textured foliage is supplied by *Hosta x tardiana*, a diminutive gem whose perfect little leaves will last over two weeks in a decoration. Single and double dianthus mix their clove-like fragrance with the heavier scent of the roses. The whole decoration is topped off with a tuft of glaucous blue-grey grass, resembling a Regency belle's egret – a decoration of heron feathers worn in the hair for evening parties. This is one of the most durable of grasses, forming long-lived clumps of ever-grey foliage. The arching wands of flowers appear in late May and add enormously to the elegance of the spiky tufts. A perfect punctuation mark for the garden, it is blighted for me by the name *Helictotrichon sempervirens*. Its synonym *Avena sempervirens* offers a more pronounceable alternative. Perennial clumps look especially attractive under-planted

Figure 9

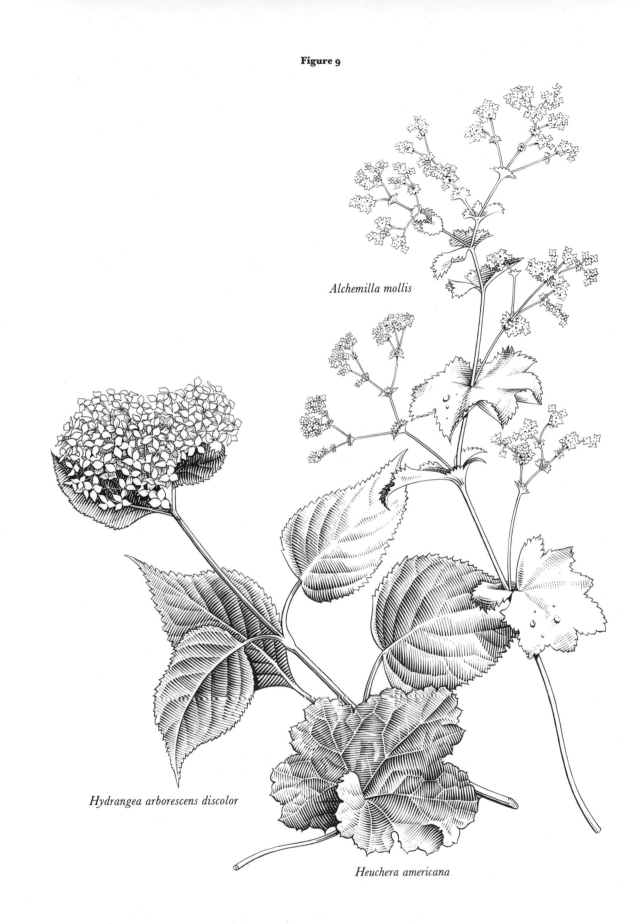

Alchemilla mollis

Hydrangea arborescens discolor

Heuchera americana

with the flowerless form of lamb's ears, *Stachys lanata* 'Silver Carpet'.

The second decoration to illustrate this chapter brings us up to date with modern floribunda roses raised with the flower arranger in mind. The variety is 'Vesper' raised by Messrs E. B. Le Grice of North Walsham, Norfolk. This family firm has bred and introduced a great many subtly coloured roses, especially floribundas, which cater for the demands of floral artists seeking the subdued in spite of a world market that demands the over-large, over-coloured and over-garish in everything. They are to be applauded for such charming roses as 'Great News', 'Silver Charm', 'Amberlight', 'Tom Brown' and 'Vesper', to name a few. A completely new break in colour is the mahogany red of 'Jocelyn' which ages to purple-brown as the flat, double flowers expand. This rose was named in honour of Mrs Jocelyn Steward, the first Chairman of the National Association of Flower Arrangement Societies of Great Britain. An indefatigable gardener and flower arranger noted for her all-green designs, she now lives in South Africa. 'Grey Dawn' is another unique colour which has yet to prove itself here. The flowers are borne singly and in clusters and are a strange, soft grey. It will certainly require careful siting to avoid the washed-out appearance which is the criticism most frequently levelled against the use of these off-beat colours out of doors.

Of all the modern roses the floribunda 'Vesper', named after the evening star, must rate very high on my list, as its colour appeals to me enormously. The buds begin a warm yet soft orange-brown, which pales as they open. Overtones of pinky apricot develop in hot weather, like some ancient amphora of terracotta mellowed by centuries of sunshine. This variation of colour adds considerably to its charm and enables it to be mixed with both pink and orange-toned flowers, softened by grey foliage, or contrasted with lime greens and browns. In the arrangement in Plate VIII I have used it in two Italian vases of alabaster. The lowest section is separate, supported by

three swans with their necks on their breasts. I have often used a much larger and almost identical version at Badminton House for the Duchess of Beaufort. The top four sections are a separate vase and by some happy chance fit exactly inside the lower, appearing as one whole. Alabaster is a porous material and it is quite fatal to fill it with water. On one occasion a magnificent vase at Harewood House disintegrated, much to the chagrin of the arranger, who had heaped it up with glorious autumn fruits and flowers in many crashing shades of red. A flurry of handkerchiefs was produced to save the tooled crimson leather of the superb Chippendale library table, now displayed at Temple Newsam, near Leeds. This lesson has always stayed in my mind when using alabaster, and coating the interior with paraffin wax or varnish is essential. As this is not always practical, Oasis wrapped in several layers of metallic florist's foil is the method employed, thus obviating the need for free water in the five bowls. Topping up the arrangement means a judicious dribble of water daily for each piece of Oasis, and the whole decoration lasts over a week with some replacement of roses.

The setting suggests a formal and cascading style of design, to follow the fountain-like dictates of the vase. The bronze-green of the carpet and the lime-green velvet mounts of the seals preclude my favourite combination of grey-blue foliage with this rose and so a lime and moss-green scheme has been adopted. The foliage and flowers should be picked the evening prior to being arranged, to give them the essential pre-conditioning period, the secret of success with any floral design. Beginning at the top, the minute but intriguing tiny green and pink flowers of *Heuchera americana* add an airy note to the fountain. The leaves of this plant are beautifully suffused with bronze over green, the texture almost crystalline. This charming shade plant supplies summer leaves whilst the very similar tellima is gathering substance ready for the winter, when its leaves are at their best. It deserves to be more widely grown and the

Figure 10

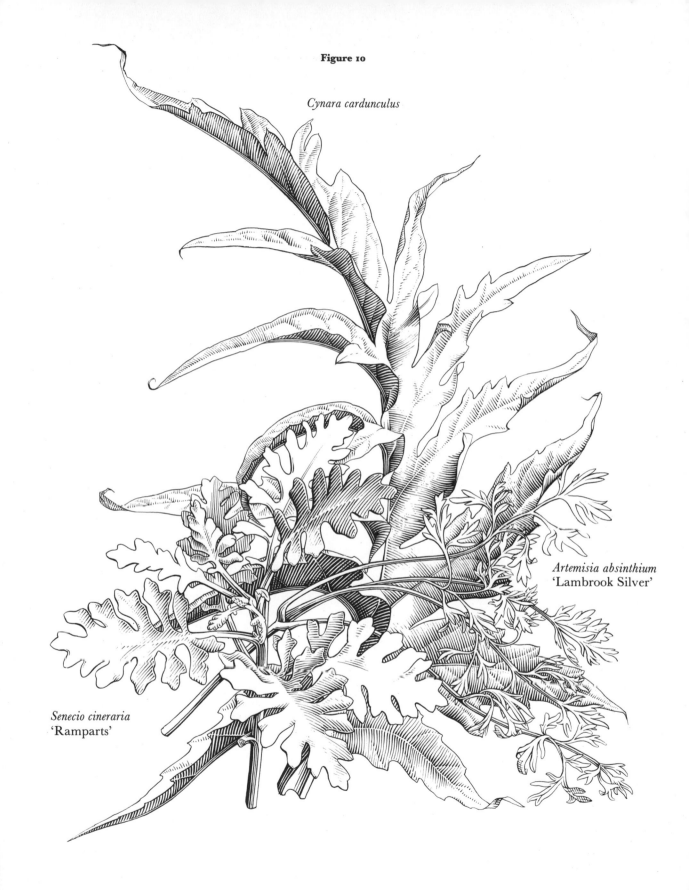

Cynara cardunculus

Artemisia absinthium 'Lambrook Silver'

Senecio cineraria 'Ramparts'

drawing in Figure 9 clearly shows its irregular outline. No two leaves are identical, and as they mature they turn a soft pink and coral similar in colour to the rose 'Vesper'. The cascade effect is continued by sprays of Lady's Mantle: *Alchemilla mollis* goes with almost everything which, together with its ease of cultivation, possibly accounts for its popularity. Here its lightness helps considerably to link the four groupings with a gentle, rhythmic flow. The hosta is the lovely golden-edged variety, which labours a little under the name of *Hosta fortunei* 'Obscura Marginata'. The prime factor in its favour is that it lasts longer in leaf colour than any other variegated plantain lily. Others may be more vivid or striking but this one retains its attractive, pale yellow edge through the season from May to October, the leaf strengthening in texture as it grows. I rarely cut it before midsummer as there are so many other hostas with lime and yellow tints to foil our flowers. A few other flowers are worked into the pattern, namely *Alstroemeria ligtu* hybrids and a small, unnamed kniphofia from a batch of mixed seedlings, neat in habit and more apricot than orange. Near the centre of each group is a spray of *Euphorbia niciciana*, one of Mrs Chatto's excellent plants. Less hardy than most euphorbias, it enjoys a hot, sunny position in the garden. The green bracts surrounding small, yellow flowers are of such intensity that the whole plant vibrates with colour, set off by cooler blue-green foliage. It lasts well as cut material and makes a long-lasting display in the garden.

The completed design displays the gradual development of the roses, which form the focal area, and echoes the colour of the curtains and cushions. The elusive colour of the walls and damask covers is taken up by the antique alabaster. A small base of moss-green velvet protects the pembroke table and adds visual weight to balance the composition.

The latest introduction to this collection of personal preferences is 'Victoriana', likely to become a favourite floribunda with flower arrangers. The colour is extraordinarily difficult to describe: it is vermilion-red on the inner side of the petal overlaid with silver-grey, this contrasting with the soft, silvery-grey reverse of the full, rounded flowers. The stature of the bush is short and sturdy, but as yet I only have it newly planted. An added bonus is its sweet perfume. I cannot wait to try it combined with grey and silver foliages.

Schools of thought vary about how to place roses in the overall design of the garden, and much depends on the house itself. Those who favour a formal treatment with beds of one variety, possibly underplanted in the spring, have a long winter period when dormant stems are all there is to see. This rigid type of design is best reserved for hybrid tea roses interplanted with standards or climbers on pillars or pergola. I find this somewhat contrived and much prefer an informal scheme, where less self-conscious roses can be interspersed with other plant associations – this helps to create living arrangements and embodies ideas for indoor decorations. The species and shrub roses with their looser habit of growth lend themselves well to this sort of artistry, and it allows infinite scope for personal taste and dexterity of inter-planting.

The line drawings accompanying this chapter include some favourite plants suitable for association with roses. These plants can be used to calm over-brilliant roses or to enliven those with off-beat colours. The plants I describe are all easy of culture and supply the arranger with indispensable cut material. Figure 10 shows three grey foliage plants in this category, each useful at a slightly different season of the year. Firstly the cardoon, *Cynara cardunculus*, a large and statuesque plant suitable for the middle or back of a border. It amazes me how often people confuse this with the globe artichoke. Careful observation shows them to be two different plants, though admittedly both are edible. In the globe artichoke, *Cynara scolymus*, we eat the flower buds. This bud is covered with rounded scales which surround the delicious inner portion known as the heart. The cardoon is rarely served as a vegetable in Britain, but in Italy the leaves

are blanched and eaten cooked. Whether grown for its handsome foliage, scaly flower buds, giant blue thistle-like flowers, or tightly packed seedheads, it is a must. The leaves are deeply incised, grey at first growing rapidly in length and changing to grey-green. Grown from seed, it takes some years to establish, but is worth the wait. The foliage is prone to wilt suddenly if cut too young and the removal of too many leaves from young plants results in a disfigured clump, so be patient. Boil the cut stem ends for one minute and then soak, but do not immerse in deep water. The flower buds can be removed on young plants to help them get established. The cut flowers dry well, and once the blue part has been pulled away after drying, a honey-gold boss of seeds remains encased in a crenellated collar of bracts.

The second plant is one of Mrs Underwood's carefully selected forms of *Senecio cineraria*. More white than silver, 'Ramparts' is a most useful foil plant. Though not considered hardy, in recent years plants have come through our relatively mild winters. Nevertheless, a stock of young cuttings is always taken as a reserve. As with all selected forms, propagation is vegetative, so do not be misled into buying the seedlings sometimes offered for sale. 'Ramparts' only lasts in water when fully mature, from July onwards, but associates well with any pastel colouring or even brilliant reds. The bright yellow flowers give it an untidy appearance, as well as weakening the effect. Nip them off as they appear on the tips of the shoots. New shoots will continue to break from the base and the whole plant can be cut down in April, if winter frosts have spared it for so long. It contrasts well with foliage of a bronze or rubiginous hue and looks especially attractive in front of *Rosa rubrifolia* or *Rosa farreri persetosa*, the latter being quite different in size and scale from other species roses. The name 'Threepenny Bit Rose' refers to the size of the tiny pink flowers which open from minute buds, quite perfect for the miniaturist. The stems are covered with fine, hairy thorns interspersed with dainty fern-like leaves

composed of seven to nine leaflets. In hot, dry weather they assume a burnished tone, contrasting well with the neatly cut, felted foliage of the senecio.

The third plant, though decorative all the year, is most useful for picking in autumn. *Artemisia absinthium* 'Lambrook Silver' owes its origin to the observant selection of Mrs Margery Fish. The foliage of this shrub is lustrous and silvery green in spring: give it a short-back-and-sides in March. The mounds of mimosa-like yellow flowers appearing in July emit a musty smell repellent to flies, which is perhaps why Wormwood was used for strewing floors long ago. After flowering, the whole plant puts forth new lacey leaves on long petioles and these are a delight to pick. They last well cut if first hardened in water and also look decorative on the plant with the second flush of September roses.

The recent hot, dry summers have tempted me to grow more grey foliage plants for they bear drought unflinchingly. They are accommodating in any season except in persistent rain, when they can look bedraggled and lack-lustre. More plants to associate with roses include the three illustrated in Figure 11. The first is biennial, seeding itself about, with disastrous results if not re-sited. The flat rosettes of felted grey leaves of *Onopordon arabicum* look fine at the edge of the border during the first year, but by the second season this six-to-eight-foot giant grows a foot a week in early summer. One or two make a most dramatic grouping at the back of a border, well staked when about three feet high. The first year leaves make useful picking material, but the beautifully flanged, silver-grey spiny stems, side leaves and flower buds require gloved handling. Once the purple thistles have set seed the plant becomes shabby and tired-looking, but dead-heading will help to delay this sad decline until September. Look about for self-sown seedlings at this time for transplanting. Seedlings moved in the spring sometimes sulk for that year and flower the next; so if it is flowering plants you are after, autumn replanting is the answer. The leaves should never be immersed in water when picked for decoration. This is bound to cause trouble later as the wet, woolly leaf base will syphon water out of the vase. It is best to remove the lower wool with a knife blade and boil the stem tip, then stand in shallow water overnight. The plants last well after this treatment, but like many grey-leaved subjects dislike water-retaining foams.

Probably one of the whitest of grey-leaved shrubs is *Senecio leucostachys*. It has an endearing habit of scrambling around other plants and filling in empty spaces most obligingly. The finely cut leaves are divided into a dozen slender leaflets, grey above and white beneath. The stems are also covered with this fine, protective, white felt, feeling like softest suede to the touch. Not considered a hardy shrub, an August batch of cuttings taken with a heel ensures a supply for bedding out in May. Plants grown in two terracotta pancheons in my cobbled courtyard have proved quite hardy, coming through several mild winters unscathed and giving pleasure in all but frost or rain. This is probably due to the much drier root conditions in the crocks plus the compactness of growth. The pale cream flowers are not unattractive, but tend to give the plant an untidy appearance and should be removed before they set seed. The plant has a natural branching habit and is much whiter in hot, dry positions. Its value as cut material is more in the category of a filler and, therefore, requires careful handling. The cut stems should be singed or boiled without delay after crushing, then stood in deep water overnight; after this it holds up well, softening hard outlines in arrangements just as it fills in gaps in the garden.

The last foliage plant to accompany roses is a low perennial carpeter, perfect for edging and spilling on to paths. The woolly, finely cut leaves of *Tanacetum densum amanum* are a delight, especially for those who appreciate the miniature. The individual leaves resemble minute, curving ostrich plumes and look as if they were cut from silver-grey velvet. Some

small rosettes appear in the cone of roses. Originally known as *Chrysanthemum poterifolium*, my form rarely flowers, which is an advantage as the blooms are unattractive and best clipped off. It makes excellent ground cover as a foil for more dominant partners.

All these plants place the emphasis on grey-green or silver-grey as being one of the most useful colours for neutralizing over-strident rose colours, or for drawing out the softer, subtle tints of the flower arranger's roses. Not all these roses are grown for their flowers: those with good fruits will be discussed in a later chapter. The only physical drawback to the rose must surely be its thorns. There must be a moral behind something so beautiful being attended by something so vicious. One species which is grown exclusively for its thorns is *Rosa sericea pteracantha*, which has large, flat, crimson thorns thickly arranged along the entire stem. Garnet red against the light, they change to the colour of clotted blood on mature wood. They are decorative either as young cut material or as dried defoliated thorns. The drying process frequently happens in an arrangement of its own accord, and the stems can be harvested when it is dismantled.

The species rose for foliage *par excellence* is *Rosa rubrifolia*, illustrated in Figure 15. The plant bears single pink dog roses in June, followed by clusters of brownish-red hips in autumn. It is indispensable as a foil to other plants and provides elegant, long sprays for cutting. The colour defies adequate description, being such a mixture of glaucous grey-green overlaid with plum and shading to maroon, in a half-and-half division of the leaflets. The plant is almost thornless and the bark suffused with a bloom which adds greatly to its elusive colouring. New shoots are ideal outline material for pedestal work. These should be crushed, boiled and then steeped in deep water, after which they will last a long time provided the tips have hardened up. Hard pruning will encourage a supply of fresh growth, with occasional bird-sown seedlings as vigorous reserves.

Figure 11

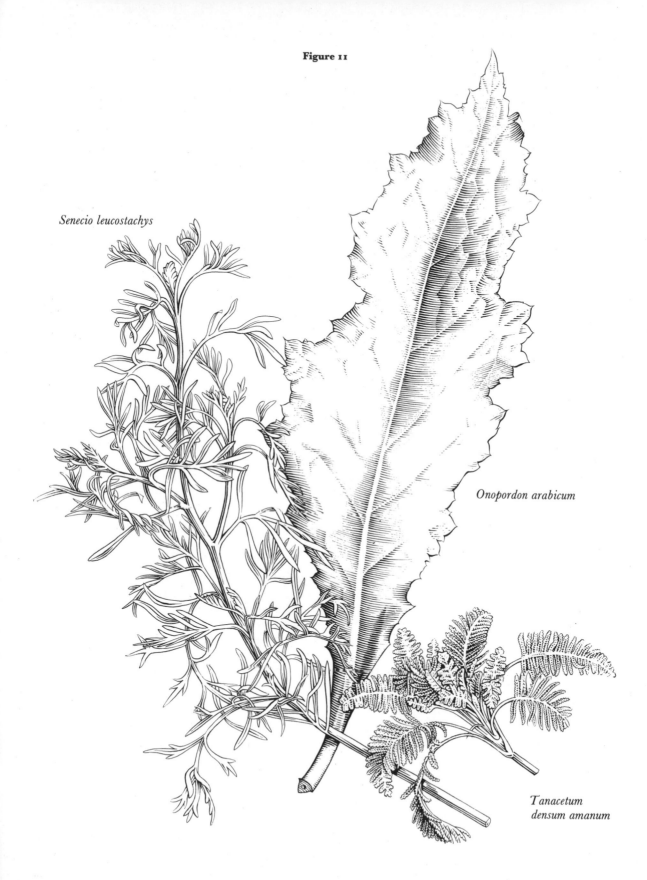

Senecio leucostachys

Onopordon arabicum

*Tanacetum
densum amanum*

5 High Summer

By July and August our gardens have reached full maturity, provided there is a constant supply of moisture. Our temperate climate and regular rainfall are something we tend to take for granted in Britain. The dire shortage of water experienced in the two hot, dry summers of 1975 and 1976 may well make us more appreciative of this precious commodity. To see our plants die and our verdant landscape wither was tragic. Flowers and foliage grown without adequate moisture make poor materials for cutting and require extra care in their conditioning.

Amongst the most useful and sought-after of flower arranger's plants are the moisture-loving hostas, three more of which appear in Figure 12, all varieties which can be relied upon to improve in quality and substance as the year progresses. Unlike the brightly coloured spring effects discussed in Chapter 3 these retain their variegated colour well into autumn, putting on a brief display of amber-yellow as they die down in October. All three are choice, the most widely distributed being *Hosta fortunei* 'Obscura Marginata'. It can be found for sale under several names arising out of its distinctive yellow leaf margin. The ovate leaves are well veined with a smooth mid-green central portion edged with an uneven band of creamy yellow. The distinguishing feature is the continuation of a fine cream hem right down the leaf stalk. For many years I simply called mine 'Yellow Edge', which describes it well. A decorative plant for open shade, the leaves will scorch badly in full sunshine in spite of moisture at the roots.

The next hosta came to me from Mrs Lilian Martin, a Scottish flower arranger with a flair for the unusual and an eye for a plant of quality. *Hosta tokadama* 'Variegata' differs from all others in that the leaf is cupped, as if the puckering along the veins prevented it from expanding fully. With the exception of *Hosta x tardiana* it is the bluest of all, with a generous overlay of lime

green which develops from the centre, extending outwards towards the blue edges. The underside is covered with a grey-blue highlighting the wavy leaf edge, especially on the pronounced lower lobes. It is a real treasure, increasing slowly in rich, deep soil. I am lucky to possess stock from the garden of Crathes Castle, Kincardineshire, given to Mrs Martin by Lady Burnett of Leys. The Japanese equivalent of this plant offered by one specialist in Britain is *Hosta tokadama* 'Aureo-nebulosa'. It is slow to settle down, but for this rarity it is worth the wait.

Quite the most ravishing of all the hosta family, to my mind, is *Hosta sieboldiana* 'Frances Williams'. I first encountered this plant at the Case Estates in Massachusetts, the botanical garden of Harvard University. It makes a large plant with all the qualities of its superlative parent *Hosta sieboldiana elegans*. Frances Williams must have been very pleased to spot this plant, first seen in Connecticut, and for it to bear her name. After a report I wrote on my garden for the December 1974 *Journal of the Royal Horticultural Society* I received the surprise gift of a small root from Jim Archibald and Eric Smith, at that time trading as 'The Plantsmen' and well known for their experience in the cultivation and breeding of this genus. From that generous start has developed a handsome clump. Several leaves appear in the decoration in Plate X. The larger leaves have an Egyptian air reminiscent of a Pharaoh's fan wielded by a Nubian slave. The leaf is rugose, blue-green in colour and the glaucous corrugations catch rain drops. The edges are broadly painted with lime green generously applied with sweeping brush strokes, and present a striking combination of contrasting colour. This plant is worth all the searching it may take to find.

White flowers are amongst my favourites and I have devoted a long border to them interspersed with grey foliage plants in the

Figure 12

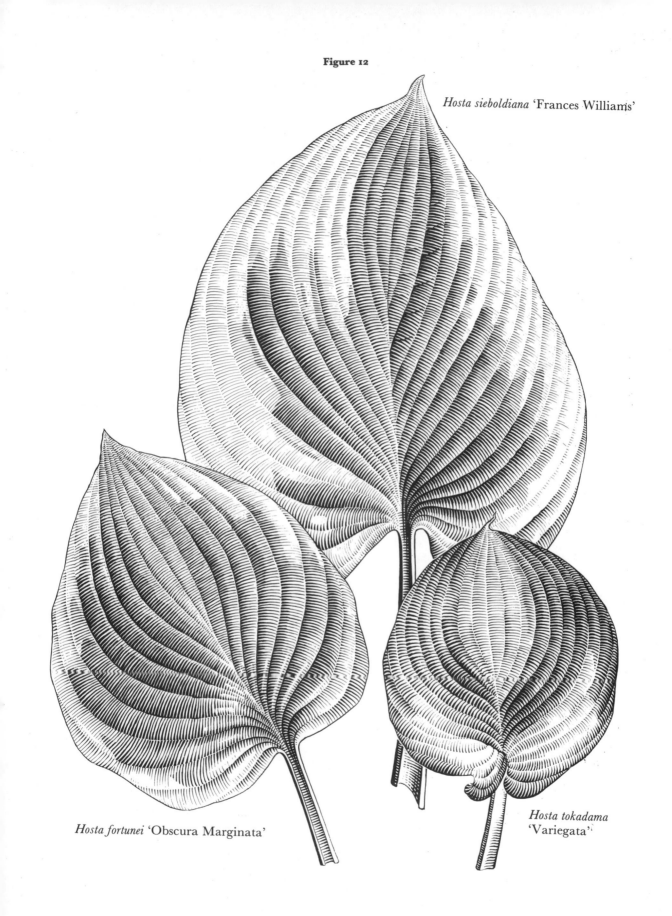

Hosta sieboldiana 'Frances Williams'

Hosta fortunei 'Obscura Marginata'

Hosta tokadama 'Variegata'

manner of Vita Sackville-West. I prefer white isolated from other strong colours in a garden. Plate IX shows a selection picked in the first week of July when hot, sultry weather suggested this refreshing combination. The container is a heavy, white marble lamp stand with ormolu base and elegant handles representing double entwining serpents, French in origin. Any white container would be good provided it allowed for a downward sweeping movement of the blossom. The mechanical support consists of a large candle cup tin firmly lashed to the lamp socket with Oasis tape and cushioned with Plasticine. A half-block of Oasis fills the tin, strapped in with more tape. To prevent any forward tilt of the tin, an Oasis pinholder is applied to the foam at the back: to put it underneath would be less effective on the gravitational pull.

A feature of the design is its apparent lightness and fluidity of line in the classical triangular style. The outline material consists of a Mock Orange *par excellence*. *Philadelphus* 'Beauclerk' makes a large bush and is, I think, the loveliest of these pineapple-scented hybrids. The single flowers are borne in great profusion on long, arching stems grown the previous year, this necessitating pruning immediately after flowering to remove weak and confused growth. Careful conditioning of philadelphus is essential for lasting success. First crush or split the stem ends and put immediately into tepid water. Remove all foliage the entire length of the stem and replace in water. The defoliating process greatly enhances the appearance of the flowers and without this treatment they will wilt. It may seem a laborious chore, but the leaves come away easily if given a gentle backward tug. After an overnight drink in a cool place they will last for almost a week if gathered in the half-open stage. This is a shrub for an open, sunny position with no special soil preferences. I grow three in different aspects, including deep shade, to obtain a succession of bloom.

The purity of the white flowers suggests the inclusion of *Lilium regale* for focal weight. One of the easier lilies to grow, it produces many heads on one stem. It is, however, the single blooms from small side bulbs which are the most useful for arrangements. The flowers have a quality and texture in harmony with the marble in the container in my arrangement, their reverse petals toning effectively with the rust-coloured curtains. It is advisable to remove the yellow pollen sacks as these burst when ripe and will stain the flowers, clothes and furnishings. By now we have a heady combination of fragrances not for the claustrophobic. Maintaining unity with the vase, creamy-white foliage increases the airy appearance of the whole composition.

A tree which can be cut at hard is certain to be welcome with those who grow to pick. Poplar trees should never be included in a garden scheme except of the most expansive kind. They sucker and run their roots in all directions creating havoc in drainage pipes or driveways. The variegated poplar is best cut back each winter and grown as a feathered standard. This hard pollarding will encourage *Populus candicans* 'Aurora' to produce side shoots ideal for cutting. The new growth is cream mottled on green, with pure cream and apricot-pink tips in June. It is difficult to condition at this stage but crushing, immediate boiling and a long soak will do the trick. By July it is more reliable if less colourful. Short sprays foil the central lilies and help to conceal the mechanics aided by leaves of *Hosta crispula*, the best of the white-edged hostas, gathered from a sheltered corner.

These are the major ingredients of the arrangement with white delphiniums and *Campanula persicifolia* 'Alba' used for height. The moisture-loving astilbes make only short-lived cut flowers but add a dainty transition from outline to focal area. Two other variegated plants add distinction, a quality necessary in any individual creation. The graceful Japanese grass *Miscanthus sinensis* 'Variegatus' delights me all summer with five-foot stems of leaves longitudinally variegated with more white than green. It forms a non-invasive clump by the pool side, creating contrast with the glossy green of *Hosta plantaginea* 'Grandiflora', and included here it helps to break any rigidity of outline. Near the centre of the arrangement are a few sprays of water figwort, *Scrophularia aquatica* 'Variegata', also illustrated in Figure 14. This striking perennial is at home by water. It sends up branching, square stems of heavily marbled cream and sage-green leaves in alternate and opposite pairs. Some people prefer to nip off the insignificant brown flowers to encourage better foliage. Watch out for caterpillars which can quickly ruin its appearance.

The after-care of the arrangement consists of a daily refill of the tin and a gentle syringing overhead with water to freshen, having first protected the furniture with plastic sheeting. The elegant pembroke table and bases of coral velvet help to balance the flowing proportions of a design suitable for a wedding or similar function.

The Sea Hollies are increasing in popularity and deserve a place in every arranger's garden. The candied roots of our native *Eryngium maritimum* were eaten as a sweet in Elizabethan times. They may be divided loosely into two groups. Those with rounded leaves borne on pedicels originate principally in Europe, whilst the American species have long strap-like leaves, barbarously serrated. Three are of outstanding value to the arranger and garden decorator.

I first encountered *Eryngium alpinum* 'Donard's Form' in the garden of the late Miss Nora Watson at Beckingham in north Nottinghamshire. She was a woman of encyclopaedic knowledge coupled with an originality easily mistaken for eccentricity, except by those who recognized it as a cover for her shyness. She endeared herself to everyone, unquestioningly bestowing cuttings and information on all who asked. Some undoubtedly took advantage of her generosity. My visits to her and her centenarian mother required stamina as she rarely retired before 6 a.m. Dinner was frequently at midnight, so the small hours became her evening, spent discussing the merits of various plants. A voracious reader, she was well informed on a wide variety of subjects, plants being her abiding passion. I

cannot look at the steely-blue flowers of this eryngium without recalling those happy meetings.

The central flower cone opens first, followed by the side buds, each surrounded by layers of finely divided blue bracts like a collar of metallic lace, yet soft to touch. As the side branches develop, the whole inflorescence becomes suffused with this unusual blue. They all enjoy full sunshine in an open, well drained position.

Miss Willmott's Ghost is the strange name given to *Eryngium giganteum*, a plant for the moon-lit garden. The collar or involucre is silvery green, spiny-sharp and beautifully wrought. A plant associated with Miss Ellen Willmott, it dies after flowering. The self-sown seedlings appear up to eighteen months later. This can result in some frustrating gaps in planting-schemes. More than once I have been surprised by their sudden reappearance after a long absence. Dried flower heads of this eryngium appear in Plate XIV.

The best of the three in Figure 13 will surely become the one species arrangers will covet most. A fine clump, with leaves like a cross saw, has established itself against a broad stone step in full sun. From a bold rosette appear several heads of shining, platinum-coloured flowers, individually bigger than the two other species and less branching. The flower is well named *Eryngium proteiflorum* for its long, pointed bracts of a lustrous sheen suggest at once those strangely attractive South African endemics. It lasts in beauty many weeks and produces drooling noises from garden visitors but claims more than admiration from those who come too close. The dried heads are disappointing and perhaps glycerining might be better. Possibly in a desire to get the best of both worlds I have left it over-long before harvesting. This plant is destined to be a show stopper and is sometimes sold under the name 'Delaroux'. I am indebted to Mrs Doris Horne for adding this peerless solo performer to my garden scene.

With an almost uncanny regularity, certain Red Hot Pokers put forth their flowers at the same time each year. August is the month for *Kniphofia* 'Little Maid', raised by Mrs Beth Chatto and resembling the taller 'Maid of Orleans' but looking neater and more compact. It has grassy foliage from which rise slender two-foot stems half-covered with a head of creamy-white tubular florets set off by a lime-green tip. These are borne in profusion on established plants. They last for a long time when growing or as cut flowers, and are featured in Plate X. As with all kniphofia, the cream pokers have a habit of turning upwards in water. There is no cure for this except to readjust them. For this reason they are arranged in wire netting in a wide bowl of speckled cream stoneware by David Lloyd-Jones. The simplicity of the container harmonizes with the informal asymmetric design, placed at one side of the table and balanced by the light bracket.

The tallest placements are elevated in tubes bound to canes and are put in first. These consist of kniphofia, butterfly gladioli and lesser burdock. *Arctium minus* is a common wayside weed. The maroon burs persist after it has flowered. As children we delighted in throwing them at each other. Here their colour picks up the maroon specks on the *Lilium auratum* and the pattern of the carpet. Flowing from top left down to lower right are tendrils of *Lonicera tragophylla* in a subtle blend of maroon and glaucous blue. This yellow-flowered, scentless honeysuckle is a plant of great beauty, especially if grown shaded by a wall of antique brick.

The spectacular leaves of *Hosta sieboldiana* 'Frances Williams' consolidate all ingredients and link the lime and cream of the pokers to the muted duck-egg blue of *Hydrangea x macrophylla*. These heads are beginning to turn from blue to green, and if defoliated will dry naturally in the decoration. Two sprays of variegated ivy *Hedera colchica* 'Dentato-variegata' used on the right carry through the movement and add their yellow to the lime green of a few astilbe leaves used to frame the lilies. These large flowers of the sacred lily of Japan are placed in individual glass tubes. I find this the most practical way of using a many-headed spray, especially as they face in opposite directions when used entire. The Regency table of simulated rosewood has an ogee pedestal poised on a quadruped base. This open base relates to the other areas of space within the framework of the setting, creating what we call scale: too large or too small a decoration would immediately upset our sense of proportion.

Water in the garden in proportionate quantity to its size adds a fourth dimension, attracting wild life in the shape of birds, animals and insects. No other feature gives me as much pleasure as our pond, with a daily routine of fish-feeding during summer. It also provides an area of marginal planting for some of the most decorative of plants including astilbes, iris, hostas, rheums, rodgersias and peltiphyllums. Aquatics such as bulrushes, cyperus and waterlilies draw us to the brink. The three plants in Figure 14 are all worth a place in such a scheme and are useful for cutting. The bold foliage of *Ligularia dentata* will add a dramatic note, but the form 'Desdemona' has refinement plus the added attraction of mahogany red on the undersides of the leaves. The large, rounded leaves borne on stout stalks are entire, with a finely serrated edge. The orange daisy-type flowers are crude in colour but the dandelion clock seedheads which follow will preserve for dried arrangements if sprayed with hair lacquer. Young leaves are prone to attack from cut leaf beetles and slugs, which revel in the moist conditions. As the plant seeds itself freely, less colourful progeny must be rogued out to preserve a deep-coloured strain. As cut foliage it must be picked when mature, boiled and soaked. It is most useful when a large maroon-backed leaf is needed. It associates well with cut sprays of *Berberis thunbergii* 'Atropurpurea', the spiky leaves of *Cordyline australis* 'Atropurpurea' and *Sedum maximum* 'Atropurpureum' which all share the same maroon-bronze colouring.

Close by the pond grows the variegated form of water figwort in a pleasing association of contrasting shape and colour with the ligularia.

Figure 13

Eryngium alpinum 'Donard's Form'

Eryngium giganteum

Eryngium proteiflorum

Already discussed earlier in the chapter, the winter rosettes of *Scrophularia aquatica* 'Variegata' remain above ground unlike the wild figwort, *Scrophularia nodosa*, a name by which it is still erroneously known. The slender reedmace, *Typha gracilis*, grows in water. The reedmace family have been known so long under the name bulrush that the latter has become fixed in the public mind, which is most confusing as it is not a rush. There are three species growing in my pond and one more, an uninvited arrival, almost took over. The wild greater reedmace, *Typha latifolia*, is only for lakes and ponds in the wilder landscapes, for it rapidly increases by long, underground stems. I was at first flattered by its self-sown appearance in our modest pool, but later regretted its intrusion. The miniature reedmace, *Typha minima*, resembles a fat, brown cocktail sausage on a foot-long stick. Confined to a small, stone tank it is charming and would be a good choice for those with only limited space. Much larger but still useful is *Typha angustifolia* with slender brown fruits on five-foot stems. Between the two comes the plant most useful to the arranger: *Typha gracilis* lives up to its name with graceful, slender foliage and delightful pencil-slim fruits. When the male portion of the flower blows away the green velvet fruit carried on three-foot stems will begin to change colour. This is the right moment to harvest the fruits, which will dry out slowly, remaining dark, compact and brown for many years. The all too frequent question, 'Why did my bulrushes burst open?' occurs because people will leave them to get too ripe before harvesting. Once the natural cycle is completed they will burst, especially when introduced to a warm, dry atmosphere.

In Chapter 4 three plants are illustrated in Figure 9 for use with roses in arrangements. By far the best known and most popular plant of the three is *Alchemilla mollis*, commonly called Lady's Mantle. It is one of the easiest of herbaceous perennials and seeds itself about so freely that it can become a nuisance. The rounded, pleated leaves are soft green and downy with a finely serrated edge which to my eye strengthens its likeness to a high, ruffed Elizabethan collar. Each leaf holds a glistening bead of moisture after heavy dew or rain. The flowers are carried in fluffy panicles consisting of dozens of tiny lime-green florets. These appear from June onwards and the regular removal of faded sprays will encourage a succession of blooms throughout the summer. Beloved of all flower arrangers, it is useful when cut as filler material. A word of caution here. Like all fillers it can be overdone in an arrangement and used so profusely that the individual shapes of the bolder items it is intended to unify become blurred in a sea of foaming lime greenery, rather in the same way that florist's carnations used to be smothered in a cloud of white gypsophila. One of my favourite maxims to anyone with a tendency to over-stuff their arrangements is, 'Leave space for the butterflies'. In other words, allow every flower and leaf sufficient space to show itself in the overall pattern of the design. It is the area of space surrounding each individual item that gives it value. For the same reason, plain-coloured walls and unpatterned fabrics make the best foil for arrangements. If the patterns of our flowers have to compete with each other as well as a mass of background distractions, much of their beauty will be lost. Alchemilla is useful because, like all lime greenery, it has a catalysing effect on other colours – even pale pink and pale yellow look well together if fused by its inclusion.

The second plant is the dainty perennial *Heuchera americana*, also known as *Heuchera richardsonii*. This is a relatively new addition to my garden and quickly endears itself with leaves of great beauty plus diminutive sprays of flowers on wiry stems. As cut material the leaves last two weeks or more in water. This heuchera is another of Mrs Chatto's unusual plants and is aptly described in her informative catalogue as having 'leaves of glistening silky texture in a harmony of warm browns and tan with strange green and brown flowers'. Not unlike a tellima in leaf shape as already stated, its texture is smooth and glabrous rather than hairy. The wavy, waffled margin to the lobed leaves adds to its interest. It

Figure 14

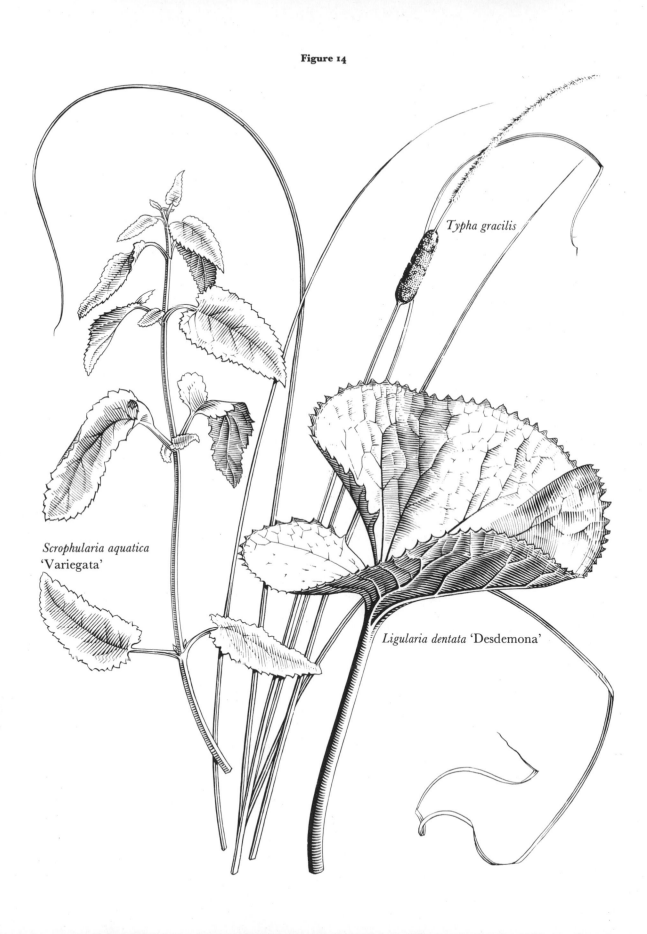

Typha gracilis

Scrophularia aquatica
'Variegata'

Ligularia dentata 'Desdemona'

prefers a cool, shady site with moist, leafy soil and like many heucheras the clumps may be divided in early autumn more successfully than in a cold spring. The late Sybil Emberton makes no mention of this modest little plant in her invaluable book *Garden Foliage for Flower Arrangement*,* so I suspect she was not acquainted with it. This is a pity because it would have delighted her. A sensitive and discerning plantsman, Mrs Emberton will always be remembered by her many admirers with respect and affection. Our collaboration together on floral projects always made me acutely aware of her knowledge and my lack. She had a real feeling for plant material. Her gentle manners and self-effacement set the seal on many friendships and her attention to detail was for me the hallmark of her genius.

I have kept *Hydrangea aborescens* subsp. *discolor* until last because it comes into a category by itself. I have known this shrub for many years as *Hydrangea cinerea* 'Sterile', but the supplement to the *RHS Dictionary of Gardening* states the former to be the correct name. I grow both *Hydrangea arborescens* 'Grandiflora' and *Hydrangea arborescens discolor* and the difference lies in the shape of the flower head and the slightly downy underside of the leaves of the latter. It makes a twiggy bush about five feet high, preferably in a shady spot. The flower heads are a rounded mass of tightly packed sterile bracts. They open a deep, fresh green, always attracting interest and comment in a decoration. As the flower heads expand they turn to palest ivory and are useful at this stage in late summer for green and white arrangements adding a subtle note to soften the hardness of all-white flowers. As the corymbs age the bracts turn over and become a mossy green, eventually drying on the plant to pale biscuit brown. As with all hydrangeas the heads last better if the foliage is removed, the stem ends are crushed and the whole head immersed in water for an hour. Flagging or limp material can be placed in shallow, hot water and then soaked.

August is one of the few times in the year when we can pause to rest and enjoy our labours.

This affords us the opportunity to study the progress of new planting-schemes and to take note of what needs to be changed during the next dormant season. Many routine jobs must still be carried out, especially dead-heading, to encourage a second crop of bloom. This is the right time to harvest everlasting flowers and to collect seed heads for dried arrangements. The preservation of freshly cut mature leaves can also be carried out by the methods described in Chapter 7. Each plant has its own time for gathering to be dried. The process begins in May with the flower heads of grasses and progresses throughout summer and autumn.

One flower that is often gathered too late is the helichrysum, together with other annual flowers of a straw-like texture, such as anaphalis, acroclinium, rhodanthe and xeranthemum. It is useless to wait until the flowers have opened to display their yellow centres. Yet how often do we see them offered for sale long past their best, the whole plant pulled up and dried.

There are many new strains of *Helichrysum bracteatum*, the annual strawflower, with softer colours than the usual garish hues. The ivory white and warm coral are the colours I prefer, but it is usually necessary to grow a mixed batch of seedlings to secure some off-beat colours. Pick them in dry weather as the outer circle of petals is expanding, leaving a half-inch stem so that the side buds and lateral shoots can develop. Once the crown bud has been severed the plant will branch with many smaller heads to give a succession of bloom. Because of this growth-habit harvesting becomes a regular weekly job. The number of flowers ready for picking will steadily increase as the plant continues to develop. The flowers must be wired the same day whilst the stem is still juicy and penetrable. Insert a ten-inch-long 22-gauge florist's wire up the stem and just into the base of the seed-box situated above the neck of the flower. Care should be taken not to insert the wire so far that it later projects from the centre of the petals. The flower will dry on the wire and hold so fast it will be inseparable.

The instructions frequently offered are to push

* Faber & Faber, London, 1968.

the wire through the head and hook it over then pull it back into the crown of the petals. Not only is this an unsightly method, it is also unnecessary. Open dried flowers sold with shrivelled stems can only be wired this way, but they look ugly and faded. The secret of the process I recommend is that the juice remaining in the seed box and stalk causes the iron wire to rust slightly and a strong union is forged between the flower and the wire. Stand the wired heads in jam-jars to dry out. The flower heads will expand and any over-blown samples will discolour and may as well be discarded. Massed in copper dishes they look effective.

Helichrysums can also be wired into long sprays by the method described for the mounting of skeletonized leaves in Chapter 7.

It is hard to imagine how much we shall prize these gleanings later in the year, when all around us the lushness of summer lulls our senses. It is easy not to realize, when all the trees are still green with leaves, how precious will be the preserved sprays of foliage usable all winter.

6 Autumn

Autumn begins quietly, imperceptible but for the stillness of September mornings as nature holds its breath, to pause at the crowning of the year. Heavy dews spangle a myriad cobwebs spun overnight. The unmelodious song of the robin pierces the silent garden with a hint of melancholy. The woods and hedgerows wear a diadem of golden leaves studded with acorns, chestnuts, crab apples, wild plums and rose hips, jewel-bright. Veiled with mist, summer prepares to die in a crescendo of brilliant colour. This is a time to take stock, looking back on sunlit days and gathering in our treasure before frost and damp lay claim.

In the garden the second flush of roses adds to the brilliance of dahlias and chrysanthemums, with colours more rich than summer's. As a bonus come blooms to surprise us with their false spring. The nerines of South Africa throw up crystalline sugar-pink flowers from sun-baked bulbs along with crimson spikes of schizostylis. The single and double colchicums push forth their naked beauty in lilac and white alongside the more delicate autumn crocus. By now many foliage plants lack lustre while others compensate, reaching sufficient maturity to be reliable for picking.

Maroon and bronze-coloured foliages are especially effective as a foil for pale colours. Three plants in Figure 15 fit this category. *Berberis thunbergii* 'Atropurpurea Superba' is the largest of the Japanese barberries recommended for picking, reaching twelve feet in height and as much across. The individual leaflets are poised on arching stems backed with triple thorns, the only drawback. Young growth does not last when cut unless crushed, boiled and soaked; remember to remove all lower thorns with a sharp knife or rose thorn strippers. The yellow flowers appear in May and combine well with such tulips as 'Scaramouche' and 'Absolome', both having off-beat maroon and lemon-yellow petals. By August the berberis lasts well and also takes glycerine solution.

Several other varieties of *Berberis thunbergii* are worth growing for garden decoration as well as for picking. *Berberis thunbergii* 'Rose Glow' has cream and pink variegation over maroon which in encouraged by full sunlight and hard pruning. *Berberis thunbergii* 'Atropurpurea Nana', with reddish leaves, makes a dwarf bush as the name implies and is useful as a low hedge plant. Slow growing but outstanding is the golden-lime colour of *Berberis thunbergii* 'Aurea', a fairly recent introduction. A group of this shrub underplanted with bronze bugle, *Ajuga reptans* 'Atropurpurea', makes a striking living arrangement.

Other shrubs with claret or maroon-red leaves are the purple forms of *Cotinus coggygria*, still listed in some catalogues as *Rhus cotinus*. The Smoke Bush gets its name from the fluffy panicles of seedheads which cover an established plant in late summer. It looks most effective if viewed against evening light. The dark-leaved form I grow is *Cotinus coggygria* 'Nottcutt's Variety' – thriving in any open, sunny position, it looks especially good interplanted with grey artemesias and the maroon-flowered *Pennisetum orientale*, a grass of great autumn beauty illustrated in Figure 17. As cut material cotinus should be crushed, boiled and soaked and is only reliable when mature. By far the most important of the three is *Rosa rubrifolia*, an indispensable species mature from June onwards. Described in Chapter 4, it combines well with the other two in a planting-scheme or arrangement, especially if grey or glaucous leaves are introduced.

Harvest time gives an opportunity for many exuberant floral creations, especially in country churches where, irrespective of ability, everyone lends an eager hand. The effect is homely and unrestrained, fitting the joy of the occasion. The decoration in Plate XI is inspired by this season

Figure 15

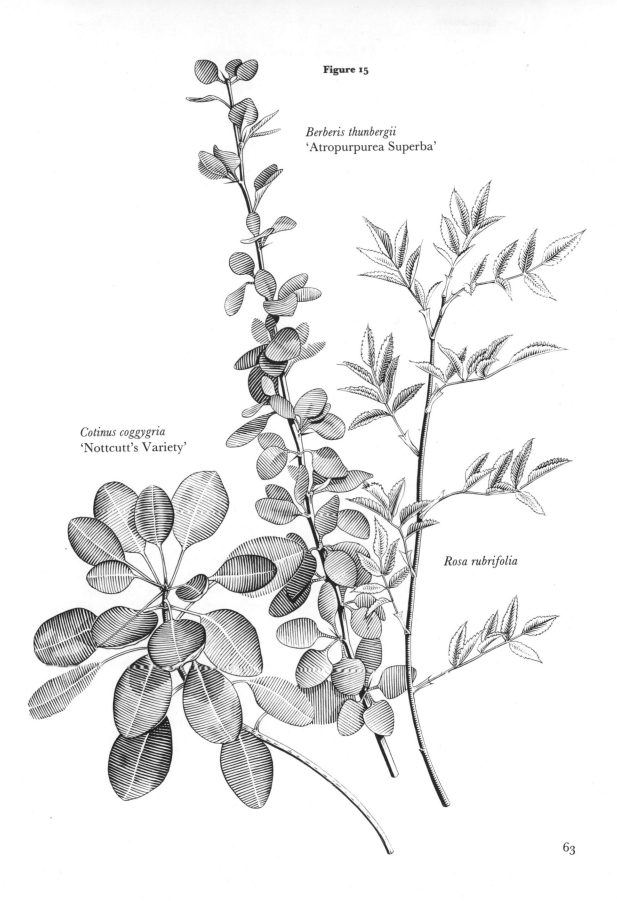

Berberis thunbergii
'Atropurpurea Superba'

Cotinus coggygria
'Nottcutt's Variety'

Rosa rubrifolia

63

of gathering-in. Assembled on an old wooden table are some ingredients for a harvest supper party arranged freely in a setting of home-spun simplicity. The triadic colour-scheme of golden tan to orange, lime green and lilac-purple is set off by the rough textured, whitewashed walls of the barn. The corn dollies worked by Brian Withill are traditional symbols of harvest home. The story of the corn dolly is an ancient one and many myths surround this traditional offering to the goddess of the grain.

The atmosphere of rustic casualness belies the sturdy mechanics employed to anchor every placement. Home-grown strings of onions are firmly thumb-tacked to the table and the wooden milk sieve, used in cheese making, is propped against wooden blocks. The two-gallon stoneware jar is raised to create an important focal pivot contrasting by its smooth texture and colour with the worn table and ladle. Repetition of this rounded form begins on the lower left with the pumpkin and rises diagonally through ladle, sieve, jar and riddle to the top right of the composition, creating a pattern but avoiding monotony by the use of a variety of appropriate accessories.

The plant material consists of a green kniphofia, dahlia 'Blue Danube', tan chrysanthemums, ligularia daisies, acanthus, *Vitis vinifera* 'Purpurea' and long trails of green Love-Lies-Bleeding, *Amaranthus caudatus* 'Viridis'. A feeling of fluid line is increased by the trails of golden hops, *Humulus lupulus* 'Aureus', with gentle tendrils leading the eye to different areas of the still-life composition. This use of fine lines within a profuse mass is an optical aid frequently employed by the Dutch painters of the seventeenth century.

The focal area consists of massed and weighty fruits of gourds, pumpkins, patty-pan squash, kohl rabi, Indian corn, marrow and celery. This heaviness is relieved by the curve of dried opium poppy heads, *Papaver somniferum*, and dried bottle gourds ending in the spiral corn dollies. The passage of time is subtly suggested by the inclusion of the scythe, its worn handle acting as

a path to link the upper and lower portions of the composition.

This profuse design could be adapted in many simpler forms for the entrance porch of a church at Thanksgiving, for a Halloween party buffet or harvest supper. Unity of idea is important when including accessories; here all have rustic origins combined with home-grown, outdoor flowers to create a natural harmony. Exotic foliage or hot-house blooms would at once strike an incongruous note. The flowers are arranged in shallow pie-tins with heavy pinholders under Oasis anchored with tape. Fruit and vegetables are kept clear of moisture to avoid their rotting. The colchicums' fragile stems are held in a cone of water as they crumple if pushed into foam.

Of garden merit are the rodgersias which are endowed with that air of refinement found in so many Chinese plants; outstanding in beauty is *Rodgersia pinnata* 'Superba', a moisture-loving plant related to the astilbes and illustrated in Figure 16. The five-lobed, digitate leaves emerge in May, unfurling deep bronze and finely creased like crinkled leather. Rose-pink flowers follow, arranged in loose panicles, but do not last as cut material. The reason for growing this aristocratic plant is its fine seedheads which persist into winter. These are of ox-blood red and may be gathered and dried in September. The leaves add distinction to a foliage group, but do not last unless well soaked and mature. The plant develops slowly by underground shoots, enjoying cool, rich soil with constant moisture. The horse chestnut-like leaves of *Rodgersia aesculifolia* are coarser, larger and less bronze; *Rodgersia tabularis* has umbrella-like leaves similar to *Peltiphyllum peltatum* but paler green, papery and prone to sun-scorch. They all make an impressive sight beside water.

For an entirely different position are the sun-loving sedums. In *Sedum maximum* 'Atropurpureum', the whole plant is dark maroon and thrives in a hot, dry position. The succulent leaves and stems end in a head of brownish-pink flowers which take until August to develop. They last a long time as cut material, adding a

distinctive note to any group. This is a slow-growing plant, but once established several clumps look well associated with the blue-grey grass *Helictotrichon sempervirens*, and *Stachys lanata* 'Silver Carpet'. It also combines well with the shrubs already described in this chapter. These plant associations gain maximum impact if planted boldly with as many plants of one type as space will allow.

The third plant in Figure 16 is a climber originating from Japan. Several vines recommend themselves for flower arranging, the most dramatic being *Vitis coignetiae*. The young leaves, which open with a pink tinge, look attractive when trained against an old brick wall. The main display comes in autumn when the handsome green leaves with their brown suede-like undersides turn yellow, scarlet and crimson. This effect is short-lived, but worth waiting for, and at this stage the leaves last well if used individually. They also press attractively for plaques and pictures of dried plant material. Long sprays with tendrils do not last even when boiled and soaked, but as this is the largest-leaved of the hardy vines it creates great contrast of foliar form in the garden, scaling trees and walls to sixty feet or more if not checked.

Autumnal colour in foliage is caused by a reduced flow of sap as a result of the advent of frost or colder temperatures. This change indicates that the leaf is dying, and therefore such material will only be short-lived when cut. Heated rooms and the drier atmospheres of the house tend to accelerate this process. However, in spite of the ephemeral quality of tinted leaves, many seedheads, berries and fruits compensate by their long-lasting qualities. Added to this, evergreen leaves are at their best, as yet unblemished by frost and wearing their new-found armour of glossy green, especially the ivies. A decoration employing these three ingredients appears in Plate XII, created for a small bedroom where the colour-scheme dictates this complementary harmony of orange and green. The room has pale green walls, a perfect foil for all colours; glazed chintz curtains and a coverlet in a design of birds of paradise combining coral, beige, browns and several greens; and a beige fitted carpet. Small antique pieces of furniture reinforce the traditional setting. Almost always we can look upon the flower arrangement as the final embellishment of a room, designed with its colour-scheme in mind, the occasion for which it was created and the function of the furniture upon which it stands. It is, therefore, vital to create a flower arrangement *in situ*, for only then will it marry with its setting.

Here the confines of a small serpentine chest of drawers, measuring only eighteen by thirty-six inches, dictates a small design. The area is dominated by the imposing French marble and ormolu vase converted into a lamp. The polished crystalline composition of the stone, flecked with grey and green, at once excites the imagination to search for similar textural qualities in plant material. The lamp shade of dark green *moiré* silk completes the composition and adds a note of almost Napoleonic masculinity. The chest, the lamp, the fabrics, all create the mood of the decoration which, whilst appearing loose and free-flowing, has been governed by the assimilation in my mind, almost unconsciously, of the overall ambience of the room. Once the arranger can reach this stage his work becomes less affected and self-conscious and merges easily into the décor of the room. For practical reasons the container is a shallow aluminium pie-tin filled with Oasis and back-weighted with an Oasis pin-holder. The tin stands on a small, rectangular bottle-green tray to give added protection to the antique surface of the mahogany chest.

The plant material consists of autumn foliage, long-lasting berries and evergreen leaves, all excellent plants for the arranger's garden. Three heads of *Eryngium proteiflorum* immediately command our attention with their distinctive form and extraordinary colouring. Already described in Chapter 5, this Mexican sea holly revels in the hot, dry conditions of stony places and astonishes with three crops of flowers in a growing season. The polished steely involucre surrounding the central cone relates beautifully to the flecks of crystal in the marble. These autumn flower heads take longer to develop and retain their iridescent platinum quality until spoilt by snow or frost, giving many weeks of pleasure. As a foil to this focal material *Begonia rex* leaves from the greenhouse add another metallic texture. The sheen of the leaves of silver and green is emphasized by a darker green border. These leaves resent Oasis and are arranged in small phials of water pressed into the foam and topped up individually. They repay this effort by lasting many weeks if picked from a sturdy plant in good health. Other dark green leaves to the centre left are those of our native *Helleborus foetidus*. Almost black-green leaves are few in the garden and these handsome, deeply divided evergreens have a metallic patina like unpolished bronze, finely cast, sombre and imposing. The fact that they are so long-lasting makes them one of my favourite leaves. A few marbled leaves of hardy *Cyclamen neapolitanum* and trails of variegated ivy complete the evergreen interest. *Hedera helix* 'Glacier' is one of the daintier cultivars with white-edged leaves overlaid with variations of grey and green. It occasionally puts forth all-cream sprays which add distinction to an arrangement. It is slow-growing and easy to keep pace with out of doors.

Near the centre of the decoration are the ferny, silver leaves of *Artemisia absinthium* 'Lambrook Silver', selected by Mrs Fish from a batch of seedlings. The wild forms of Wormwood are not nearly so attractive and the musty-smelling flowers are of little appeal. It is in autumn, when the faded flowers have been removed, that it reclothes itself with shining, silver-green leaves the colour of a celadon vase, equal in lustre to the spring display. This cultivar deserves to be more widely grown, but it is not easy to propagate which may account for its scarcity. Few plants can be more beautiful in leaf as a soft foil to other bolder leaves or flowers. Pressed individually they are useful for dried pictures under glass and retain their silky sheen for many years.

So much for the green material in Plate XII. The autumn-tinted leaves of *Azalea mollis* help the gradual transition and introduce a note of orange-red together with two small, umbrella-like leaves of *Peltiphyllum peltatum*, a waterside saxifrage from California. This imposing plant has leaves like an inverted parasol and holds water prettily after rain. The leaves colour well and although the starry, pink flowers come before the leaves, they are an added attraction in spring. It dies back to a fleshy, creeping rhizome.

The berries in the decoration consist of rose hips, Bittersweet and wild iris together with a Virginia Creeper with blue-green berries. By far the most colourful are the clustered pods filled with orange seeds of *Iris foetidissima*, our native Gladwin. This accommodating plant will grow in any odd corner and produce fat clusters of fruits which should be harvested whilst still green and on the point of bursting. These can be hung up or laid flat to dry and open in a warm, airy place. A good squirt of aerosol glue or hair lacquer spray will help to prevent the ripe seeds from scattering. Unfortunately this process does dull their lustre somewhat. The best form to grow is one sometimes called the 'Chinese Form' but more correctly known as *I. foetidissima* 'Citrina' on account of the yellow and pale mauve flowers. The seed pods are much larger and more showy with longer, evergreen leaves useful for winter decorations.

The trailing vines of orange seeds on the lower left and top right are those of Bittersweet, *Celastrus scandens*. Although introduced as long ago as 1736 this hardy and rampant climber is rarely seen in British gardens. Possibly we do not grow it in Britain because of our colder, wetter autumn, but in the eastern states of North America it is one of the most familiar sights, festooning hedgerows and sold in bunches on the roadside and at farm stores. Happily some garden clubs in the USA discourage this wholesale slaughter by putting it on their conservation lists where it occurs less abundantly. The trails of orange seeds occur

66

Figure 16

Rodgersia pinnata 'Superba'

Sedum maximum 'Atropurpureum'

Vitis coignetiae

along the vine and are offset by yellow valves. These few sprays were gathered at Cape Cod, where it grows plentifully, together with the blue-green berries of *Ampelopsis cordata*, used here defoliated.

Several roses are grown exclusively for their decorative hips or heps and perhaps the best of these for a small garden is *Rosa moyesii* 'Geranium', a more compact form selected at Wisley Gardens in 1938. The bottle-shaped hips are on the lower right of the illustration. They are at their best in August and September, but were kept for this illustration in water for a month into October, by which time the foliage had fallen away. Few birds can resist these succulent fruits. Other rose hips include the dainty sprays of *Rosa multiflora* and the redder-orange fruits of *Rosa pomifera* 'Duplex', the semi-double Apple Rose. The gold watch and chain are included to give a sense of scale to the composition. They have sentimental value in that they were given by my great-grandfather to my maternal grandmother and worn by her on her wedding day in 1886. As with the scythe in Plate XI, the passage of time at this fleeting season is suggested by this personal memento.

Autumn may linger into November, depending on the weather and the location. Given fine, dry days this is a good time to divide and replant perennial borders, whilst the ground is still warm and workable. Ideas and improvements for planting-schemes are still fresh in our minds and this offers the opportunity to correct or improve upon colour-schemes observed during the summer. Colour, form and texture, in that order, are the three most important considerations for the floral artist either indoors or out. Some people are completely insensitive to all three, but they are hardly likely to be reading this book. Let us consider first colour, for it makes the greatest impression on the eye.

In planning or redeveloping the borders at Heslington I have tried to take into account the view from each room so that the colours outside become a reflection of the interior décor. Of course this is not always possible when established shrubs planted by a previous occupant are too good to be sacrificed. Then one must work the other way and include some of that colour within the room for the period it is in bloom. This effect may sound terribly studied to the reader, but in fact it adds considerable depth to the room when the garden beyond reflects its basic colouring. Colour is a very personal matter, often a good guide to personality and character. Fortunately, we do not all like the same colours, or the degree, depth and intensity to which they are used. The room in which I write has rich crimson and gold striped walls, crimson curtains and cushions off-set by oatmeal loose covers and a beige carpet. White paintwork, black and gold lamps and accessories add up to a bold, welcoming and masculine effect. The impression it creates on visitors is quite markedly different as they react to the strong colour in different ways. This is the effect red can have on our senses, for it is never passive and has the greatest impact of all colours on our eye.

An example of interior-related planting is as follows. At the back of the border trained to the wall are Bourbon roses 'Madame Isaac Pereire' and 'Madame Ernst Calvat', interplanted with clematis 'Comtesse de Bouchaud', 'Perle d'Azur' and 'Jackmanii'. The area in front is filled with delphiniums 'Pacific Hybrid', a strain which blooms twice, dahlias 'Cheerio', 'Blue Danube' and 'Purple Gem' and floribunda roses 'Victoriana' and 'Rosemary Rose'. The front of the border contains groups of *Penstemon campanulatus* 'Garnet' and *Penstemon gloxiniodes* 'Sour Grapes', with the contrasting flower shapes of *Centaurea dealbata* and *Centaurea hypoleuca* 'John Coutts'. The latter two have knapweed-type blooms. The South African daisy *Dimorphotheca barberiae* spreads daisy-type flowers over the paved edging. All this mixture is in a hectic assortment of pink, mauve, lilac, magenta, purple and blue. They are fused together by the catalysing effect of grey and silver foliage plants, which include the great grey rosettes of *Verbascum bombyciferum*, the lacy ramblings of *Senecio leucostachys*, and explosive tufts of the blue-grey grass *Helictotrichon sempervirens*. Mats of *Tanacetum densum amanum* drape themselves on the pathway. Just as in the room the beige, white and oatmeal sober down the red, so in the border the grey foliage plants modify the impact of the flower colours.

It requires endless patience, observation and determination to put such planned planting into effect. It is like painting with plants except that the canvas and pigments are never static but constantly affected by changes of light, vagaries of weather, and the passing season as growth advances or declines. No gardener can ever suffer from boredom and no flower arranger can ever repeat the same decoration. It is this infinite variety which fascinates.

All the flowers mentioned have some blue in them as well as red. Once we can appreciate the composition of a colour then we are a long way to understanding how to handle it. Orange is the direct complement to blue, yet its inclusion in this border would look frightful because of the blue, mauve, purple, and pink-to-red spectrum. Orange is a warm, advancing colour made from a combination of red and yellow. We see much of it in autumn foliage and flowers; coral, peach, and apricot are the more subtle tints of orange moving towards orange-red in the spectrum. The effect of mixed red flowers can be greatly heightened when they are backed by maroon or purple foliage, an example being the red-leafed hedges at Hidcote Manor, Gloucestershire. If a green hedge had been used it would have had the effect of subduing the red flowers as green is the complementary balancing colour to red.

Yellow is one of the brightest and most clear-looking colours to combine with green in an arrangement. It suggests sunshine and has a cheerful, uplifting effect upon the emotions. Like all three primary colours, yellow is hard if used undiluted, but combined with paler tints of primrose and cream and used in with lemon, lime and green, it is refreshing. For a richer effect, yellows combined with gold, bronze and tan move closer towards brown and would be more subdued. Oddly enough, grey or silver foliages combine well with everything except plain mid-green. The majority of plants are green as a foil to their flowers, which may be why we are so perverse as to seek out foliages of other colours to use in our arrangements. Green can be the most restful and soothing of all colours and an interesting garden could be created entirely of greens – especially in the heart of a city. All-green arrangements have long been popular. Fortunately flower colours are rarely so concentrated that they clash, but a really carefully devised colour-scheme can be very telling.

Most people simply grow a glorious gallimaufry of plants that they like and leave it at that, lacking space or time to organize their treasures into some sort of colour-scheme. Admittedly some plants are architectural enough to stand on their own as punctuation or exclamation marks, but too many of these would spoil the effect. It is better to produce several well grown plants of each variety and group them boldly depending on the scale of the border. Autumn is the time to propagate by root division if we wish to increase the quantity of our perennial plants. Take stock of all you grow and ask yourself, does it really earn its keep, do I need it, how often do I pick it, how long does it decorate the ground it occupies? The answer to these questions may lead to some streamlining, but the important thing is to group boldly and to plant generously, trying to create as expansive an effect as the space will permit.

The scientists tell us that white is the fusion of equal quantities of all colours of the spectrum. In the garden it is the one colour which seems to stand separate from all others and this is how some of the greatest artists have handled it. The white and grey garden at Sissinghurst Castle is a famous example of this treatment. It still works, since white flowers have a luminosity which makes them poor mixers with strong colours. White and green is one of the loveliest combinations, but of course white can be mixed with pale and pastel-coloured flowers. This type of garden looks marvellous by moonlight, like a border wholly transformed by hoar frost on a winter's morning. Contrast is also important for pale and white flowers, which look twice as effective if grouped in front of dark yew hedges. This clever and carefully considered use of colour may seem irrelevant to the average garden owner and only for the great gardens. I feel it is just as important and equally applicable, for there is nothing quite so rewarding as the discovery that a mentally visualized scheme in time can become a reality. Few of us will ever become Capability Browns, but at least I hope this will tempt you to widen your horizons.

7 Dried and Preserved Plant Material

The idea of decorations created from dried and preserved material is not new, but the techniques involved and the range of materials available offer more scope than ever before. The arrangements of today bear no resemblance to the dusty over-stuffed assortments once encountered in dark parlours, which prejudice many against the acceptance of modern dried materials. The pendulum has swung so far the other way that the present-day devotee can offer us desiccated daffodils and animated roses when we least expect them. Not for me these specimens of retarded development imprisoned in glass spheres, caught like hapless insects petrified in amber. Nothing can equal the dewy freshness of a newly opened petal or the tender green of a leaf. Between these two extremes are many naturally beautiful seedheads, fruits, leaves and grasses, usable at or near the conclusion of their natural cycle.

There is much pleasure to be derived from working with home harvested and bought materials when fresh flowers are unobtainable or prohibitively expensive. With the advent of central heating few people have either time or money to create constantly fresh flower arrangements during the leaner months of the year. It is then that we derive the most enjoyment from working with our horde of carefully stored treasures, admiring their subtle colourings, varied textures and intriguing structure. Unhampered by the usual restrictions of keeping all cut ends in water or water-retaining foam, the arranger is free to experiment with decorative ideas other than arrangements in vases: wall plaques, collages, pressed flower pictures, swags and garlands all offer scope as an outlet for the imaginative and inventive.

There are many excellent specialist books on this subject which deal in detail with the techniques and skills required to achieve perfect results with home-cured ingredients. A brief synopsis of these processes is all I have space for in this chapter, but I would recommend experimentation. Trial and error is still the best way to master any subject. The commodity is so variable that one drying or preserving may vary enormously from another; do not be put off – we all have our failures. It is a year-round process, so begin to look about you for likely material.

The first and simplest process is by air drying. This consists of picking flowers, certain leaves and grasses, removing surplus foliage and tying them firmly into small, loose bunches. These can be suspended on a cord or from hooks on a rafter in a cool, airy, darkened room. Daylight will cause considerable fading, hence the need for darkness. Pick your materials when they are dry, not too far developed and free from blemishes. To avoid this developing into a florilegium, I must resist the temptation to list every plant suitable for drying, but obviously those best grown annually for this specific purpose are mentioned in most seed catalogues. The length of time required may be from several days to a week or two and frequent inspection is essential. The ties on the bunches must be tightened to prevent the contents falling to the floor as the stems shrivel.

Another method of cool air drying is to stand the plant material upright in jars or buckets, having first weighted them with stones. This can help to induce pleasing curves in the stems as the materials tend to bend over as they dry. Both methods are good for beginners and more than once I have salvaged material from a fresh display and popped it into an empty jar to dry off.

Hot air drying can be recommended for certain flowers to improve their colour retention. Delphiniums and hydrangeas are an example. A roomy airing cupboard is ideal if available. Delphiniums and larkspur should be hung upside down individually along a wire coat hanger. They will be ready in a few days. Hydrangeas should be picked when mature, crisp to the touch and slightly metallic in colour. Remove all foliage, shorten stems and crush the ends, then stand them in jam-jars containing about two inches of water. They will dry out very quickly as they drink up the water, which prevents them from shrivelling. This quick method cannot be applied to every plant as a substitute for cool air drying because it frequently results in a very brittle, over-fragile product.

Drying by pressing is another method. For more general purposes, sprays of tinted foliage, bracken and ferns may be laid between layers of newspaper and placed under unused mattresses or flat cushions. Carpets or rugs offer another possibility, but must be well away from general traffic or the over-diligent use of electric cleaners. I find a large suitcase filled with magazines makes an effective press, placed over several layers of newspaper or, better still, blotting paper. Each individual item must be laid flat with several layers of paper between each selection of items. The majority of materials used to make the arrangements illustrating this chapter, however, were preserved by other methods. Pressing destroys the three-dimensional quality of the plant and imparts a flat appearance to a free-standing three-dimensional arrangement.

The art of pressing flowers for mounting under glass demands greater skill and patience, the best results being achieved with a proper press or between layers of blotting paper under heavy books. Some of the loveliest examples I have seen of this specialized form of our art were the work of Princess Grace of Monaco. I was privileged to be shown her collection at the Palace of Monaco and was at once struck by her flair for design and sensitivity to plant material drawn from a wide source and including the simplest of wayside weeds. Examples of her work have since appeared reproduced on Monaco's postage stamps, another tribute to this amazingly talented yet so charmingly modest lady.

Whilst able to admire the skill and patience of those who preserve fresh flowers by means of dehydrating agents such as silica gel, powdered borax or fine sand, I find their ultimate life-span limited. My chief criticism is that these papery, delicate beauties tend to lack substance, and once exposed to average room temperatures, they re-absorb moisture from the atmosphere, fade and flop. They will last longer in an overheated atmosphere, but to me they seem only sere imitations of the real thing. Much more usable and reliable are reconstructed flowers contrived from seed pods, cones, winged seeds, husks and pressed petals. These can be really exciting and a vast variety are imported from East Africa and Mexico. I have had the opportunity of seeing these being made by native peoples and the process is quite fascinating. However, each to his or her own taste.

Preservation by a solution of glycerine produces the most effective way of ensuring a supply of long-lasting foliage for use at all times. The chief advantage is that it retains its original texture and three-dimensional quality. The fact that it changes from green to many shades of brown can be an added advantage, especially for use in certain colour-schemes. The most common error is to imagine that autumnal-tinted leaves can be changed by this process. It can only be effective on fresh, green material, either deciduous or evergreen, picked when the sap is still flowing. The most popular deciduous trees for preservation are beech (*Fagus sylvatica*), common oak (*Quercus robur*) and Spanish chestnut (*Castanea sativa*). Several evergreen shrubs make excellent subjects, including *Buxus sempervirens* (the common boxwood), *Choisya ternata* or Mexican Orange, *Cotoneaster salicifolia*, *Elaeagnus macrophylla* and several of the ornamental species of eucalyptus. *Fatsia japonica* leaves must be propped up to enable the solution to reach all parts of the leaf. *Magnolia grandiflora* and *Mahonia japonica* make two handsome leaves to try. The graceful ruscus, *Danaë racemosa*, and the indestructible *Aspidistra elatior* also produce excellent results.

The method is to select leaves or branches of the required type, remove lower leaves and any damaged portions. Crush the woody stem tips or pare away the bark with a knife for two to three inches. Using a wide-necked jar, make a solution of one-third glycerine with two-thirds hot water and mix thoroughly. The hot water enables the stem to drink more quickly. Stand the jar inside a deeper bucket and place the leaves or branches so that all stems are well into the mixture, in a dry dark place. Inspect the material at regular intervals as it changes colour and top up the jar with more solution. You will be surprised to find how much the foliage will drink. When the process is complete the entire leaf should have turned brown and feel supple to the touch, even slightly oily. Eucalyptus will change within a few days whilst aspidistra takes six weeks to absorb the solution, and even then may not change colour. The amount of light present will often affect this latter factor. If you require pale tan or honey-coloured leaves, stand them in full sunlight and this will cause considerable variation. If the foliage is forgotten or left for too long it may develop beads of solution on the leaf surface. This sweating process can be counteracted by exposure to heat, but there will always be a danger that over-saturated material will draw moisture from the air by deliquescence. I find material that is supple in Britain at once becomes drier and less pliant in the drier atmosphere of the United States, probably as a result of their more efficient central heating systems.

Small individual leaves can be preserved by total immersion using shallow baths of solution, in order that the whole leaf can absorb the mixture evenly. It is hard to assess exactly how long each species will take, but colour change is a guide. After a week or two they may appear slimy and unusable: gently rinse them in tepid water and if they look evenly preserved, dry them carefully for storage. This method is useful on short side shoots of bracken, *Pteridium aquilinum*, various tough ivy leaves, *Galax aphylla*, *Grevillea robusta* fronds and leaves of *Helleborus*

foetidus and *Helleborus corsicus*. Automobile anti-freeze can be substituted for glycerine, but as it is coloured it will alter the final shade of such foliage as the florist's eucalyptus, *Eucalyptus gunii*.

It is important to store all dried and preserved material carefully, away from strong light, excesses of humidity or heat and vermin. Both moths and mice are attracted to seeds containing natural oils. Glycerined materials are particularly prone to mildew and should be stored in boxes on layers of absorbent paper, especially if vegetable dye has been included in the solution, as occasionally occurs with imported leaves.

This brings me to the knotty question of dyed materials. Mercifully, a little sweet reasonableness has recently prevailed over the use of dyed or surface-coloured material. Gone are the days when the lady judge with the blue rinse wrote 'not according to schedule' about your nicely boot-polished driftwood. What is good taste to one person will be a complete anathema to another. I have deliberately included dyed plant material in both Plates XIII and XIV to illustrate the point that some colour, used with restraint, may be included, especially if it picks up a colour already present in a room. How to assemble these designs is explained in detail at the end of this chapter.

Now for some suggestions on what to grow for drying or preserving, the term usually applied to indicate the glycerine process. Ornamental grasses are increasing in popularity. They supply the arranger with graceful material suitable for lightening designs. In the garden they act as a long lasting foil to broad-leafed plants or as elegant punctuation. There are innumerable decorative species to choose from, grown for their foliage or their airy flower heads. Three favourites of varied stature are illustrated in Figure 17. The first to bloom is the perennial Golden Oats, *Stipa gigantea*, from Spain. The young plant is inconspicuous and may suffer at the hands of those misguided garden visitors who weed uninvited, so label it clearly. The leaves

73

are uninspiring, green and glossy. In mid-May it puts forth purple-bronze shoots containing the feathery flower head. By mid-June an established clump resembles a fountain of shimmering golden-green jets arching over at three feet into a cascade. From each spikelet protrudes a bristle-like appendage called an awn up to six inches long. These are attached to the inner of the three chaffy bracts which encase the flower and are called glumes. Rather technical stuff this, but it is the awns, bearded with hair in the case of *Stipa pennata*, the Feather Grass, which create such an impression. Pick and preserve it young, for once the pollen has dispersed the seeds set and the whole stem becomes dry and hay-like, incapable of drinking the solution. The plant will remain beautiful until October, for although the grain may fall out the outer glumes persist a honey beige in colour, dramatic and irresistible.

On a much smaller scale comes the Squirrel Tail Grass, *Hordium jubatum*, about one foot high. It is also called Fox Tail Barley on account of the long, silky awns which are purple on green spikelets borne in July. My original tuft was gathered from the motorway central reservation whilst held up because of an accident. It will colonize a small area with seedlings, so avoid over-vigilant hoeing. Glycerine whilst still young, for dried heads become brittle and soon disintegrate.

The third is a native of north-west India but hardy, forming tufts of soft foliage. *Pennisetum orientale* has an elusive colour when in bloom in August and September. Young flowers are soft mauve-grey set off by long, maroon awns, turning beige as they mature. It grows eighteen inches high and looks lovely when every spike is arched over with dew. It associates well with grey and wine-coloured foliage outdoors and is delightful fresh or preserved when used in dainty arrangements.

There is much wild wealth to be found throughout the British Isles suitable for drying and preserving. Pick with restraint, taking only as needed the commonest and most prolific species, in order to retain what remains of our heritage of wild flowers. Wild grasses are worth harvesting, but do not neglect to do this when they are in flower. Delaying until nature has completed the job will result in straw-like gleanings which are disappointing because of their brittleness.

In the garden the seedheads of many plants have a sculptured quality and as they are the culmination of the year's growth they can be gathered as they dry naturally on the plant, examples being *Centaurea hypoleuca* 'John Coutts', the thistle-like heads of *Carlina acaulis* and the smooth pods of *Tulipa kaufmanniana* hybrids, all in neutral colours.

The onion family offers many decorative species of ornamental value. Three widely varied species are illustrated in Figure 18. By far the easiest and most prolific is *Allium aflatunense* from China. The tightly packed, spherical umbels of lilac-mauve flowers vary in height and diameter according to the age of the bulb. This gives a useful graduation in arrangements whether used in flower, at the green-pod stage or when dry. The heads dry on the stem, ripening to reveal black seeds. Harvest in September by a gentle tug when the entire stem has dried out.

More unusual are the rocket-shaped seedheads of *Allium siculum*. The pendant flower heads on three-foot stems consist of up to thirty greeny-cream blooms striped with maroon. Beautiful at this stage, the individual heads turn upwards as they set seed like a cluster of fairy castle turrets in miniature. They turn from waxy green to honey beige. Harvest before too dry, cutting the green stem which will give off a pungent odour. They all lose this onion smell on drying.

The most spectacular head of all belongs to *Allium schubertii*, a rare and expensive bulb from Palestine, but worth searching for. The seedhead is unique, between twelve and eighteen inches in diameter. It has small lilac-pink flowers on long pedicels of different lengths. The effect is like an exploding firework. For modern and abstract arrangements it is outstanding. Unfortunately,

Figure 17

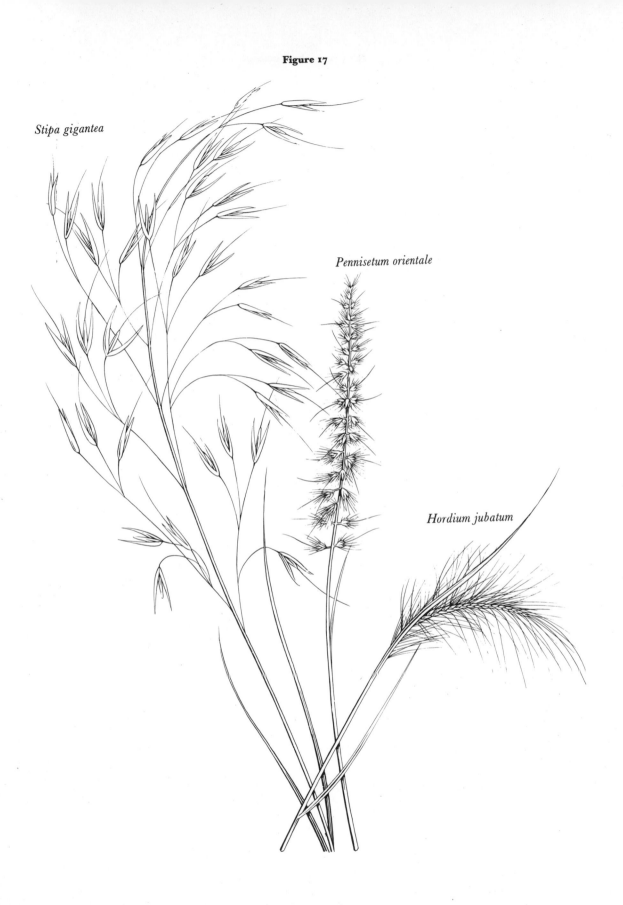

Stipa gigantea

Pennisetum orientale

Hordium jubatum

my bulbs planted in a warm, well drained site flowered once never to be seen again. Perhaps it deserves cold greenhouse over-wintering in pots to be plunged out in the sunniest border after the danger of frost is past.

Several other species of allium are worth growing for their seedheads, in particular *Allium christophii*, a ball of silvery-lilac stars retaining some colour as it dries, planted in my garden amongst bearded iris. *Allium giganteum* is the tallest and is sometimes imported from Holland as a cut flower. It lasts a very long time cut and flowers in July. For the edge of the border, *Allium karataviense* has attractive glaucous leaves veined with purple which set off the short-stemmed greyish-mauve flowers. The whole thing is subdued and delicate at every stage, especially when the seed boxes are swelling and before it dries completely. *Allium sphaerocephalum* has compact drumstick heads deeper in colour than most. They dry well if cut in full bloom in August and hung up to dry to retain their colour.

Having collected and stored our dried materials with care, there are many ways in which we can use them. Plate XIII illustrates a collage made for use as a fire screen for the room described at the end of Chapter 6. An old oval gilt picture frame measuring thirty-five by thirty-one inches is fitted with a hardboard background covered with grey-blue silk, a remnant saved from cushion making and allied to colours in the room. Strong Styrofoam forms the foundation for all the stems, a half-sphere being fixed securely to the background a little below the centre with long steel pins. First the pink grasses are inserted in a light cluster. The left-over stems are then added to suggest a bouquet. Poppy heads, sprays of beech husks and skeletonized magnolia leaves are all used to create the outline. Overlapping leaves of Bay Grape, *Coccoloba uvifera*, help to conceal the green Styrofoam. The focal area consists of three contrived flowers made from small dyed teasel-like burs grouped around a bleached centre. Dried-out gourds and three polished raffia palm

cones add visual weight and interesting textures. A small cluster of wood roses on the lower right balances two bleached ockra pods used on the left. In the centre are two tropical pods from East Africa, which introduce a brilliant note of cerise red, their natural colouring, the key to the whole decoration. Their strange, furry seeds prompt the choice of antique ribbon, worked to resemble a flat bow tying the stems together. A dried tendril of asparagus fern and the curving tulip pod add rhythmic lines to enliven the more static elements. A butterfly salvaged from a Victorian collection completes the design. As each item is clearly outlined by the background, very little material is needed, but quality is important. When not in use the frame hangs up: because of this small pins are used to prevent outer items falling forward.

Skeletonized leaves in natural and assorted colours are sold by good florists. The trouble and time involved in trying to make your own is scarcely worthwhile. Only in the tropics have I seen really successful specimens. Leathery leaves such as *Magnolia grandiflora* can be stored in screw-capped jars of rainwater stood in full sun to accelerate decomposition. The soft portion rots and has to be washed away, leaving behind the leaf veins. They can then be bleached or dried out. Commercially they are boiled in a solution of caustic soda and then scraped and washed, a slimy and laborious process requiring endless patience. On the whole it pays to buy them ready done.

When a semi-permanent decoration of preserved and dried plant material is required it is worth taking trouble to find the right materials and an interesting container, to prevent an all-brown combination from becoming monotonous and uninspiring. The pedestal in Plate XIV has originality and is an interesting object. Admittedly not everyone can find or may even want a carved and gilded Nubian. During the eighteenth century great houses, well stocked with servants, occasionally had a black page boy, some youth unlucky enough to have been shipped from Africa to Europe. The vogue is

Figure 18

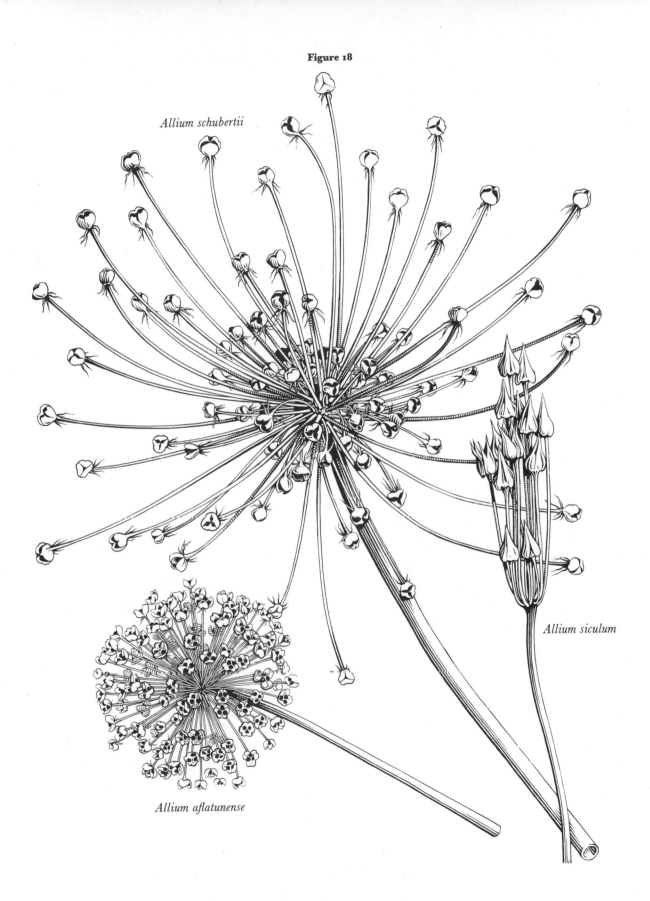

Allium schubertii

Allium siculum

Allium aflatunense

thought to have begun in Venice where they were considered a status symbol. Treated as household pets and dressed in finery, they carried the trains of ladies. British aristocrats on the grand tour were quick to copy continental ideas. When the real thing was not available, the fashion for carved wooden figures came into being. This version is five feet high, delicately carved, and beautifully dressed as a page holding a tray. The gesso inlay is finely gilded and painted in soft dark reds and blues. Many grotesque versions and imitations exist, mostly dating from after the Regency period which ended in 1820 with the close of the Carlton House era. Perhaps in some remote house is the twin brother to this fellow. They were usually carved in pairs, rarely as singletons.

Any solid stand makes a good pedestal, but obviously a really individual piece gives greater scope for distinction. The best position for any pedestal is to stand it diametrically opposite the main entrance so that the eye is carried across the room on entering. Even in a crowded gathering flowers placed above eye level will be seen and enjoyed. A column or *torchère* of wood, metal or marble is more stable than the ubiquitous wrought iron pedestal which is best reserved for church decorations. Standing in the corner of the room the blackamoor is well out of the way and acts as an interesting conversation piece.

The container for the mechanics is an old pie-tin painted mat black and weighted with lead pinholders as ballast. An oval piece of Styrofoam six inches deep is cut to fit the tin, projecting up to allow for side placements. The whole foundation is then strapped to the wooden tray. Really firm mechanics not only give the arranger confidence but pay when the decoration is to be moved for cleaning around the pedestal. Styrofoam is a strong plastic foam designed exclusively for dry materials and obtainable in green, brown or white. It is not to be confused with the softer green water-retaining foams used for fresh flowers. All are sold by good florists under brand names.

Select all the materials from your store with the design in your mind's eye, just as when picking flowers from the garden, and try to visualize the finished arrangement. In this way the required shapes and sizes come to hand including fine outline, strong focal and intermediate transitional material. Varied forms, allied colours and contrasts of texture are all needed, but a profusion of too many items leads to a confused design. Remember, real elegance of style springs from simplicity; too many mixed items will be harder to align into a cohesive whole. This is why in decorating a room already full of *objets d'art*, bibelots and furniture the most effective introduction of flowers is a vase of all one colour and one type of bloom. Few of us, however, possess that sort of interior.

In Plate XIV slender, imported water grasses form the tallest point together with a quiver of bolder, velvety grass heads. Both were bought dyed this muted ox-blood-red shade. Five leaves of preserved *Mahonia japonica* repeat a rhythmic side movement from high right to low left. In order to create unity always start high at one side and try to carry that same material across the vertical axis and down to the lower side. These leaves are also dyed, but I feel few could find them offensively unnatural, though I admit I do have a special penchant for *sang-de-boeuf* colourings. Sprays of dyed and glycerined cupressus act as a transitional filler. I have yet to discover exactly how and with what this dyeing process is achieved, but obviously it is added to the preserving solution and taken up systemically by the plant. The nearest I ever came to this was in the Lebanon where green food colouring had been added to the glycerine solution. Ivy preserved in this way was remarkably realistic, appearing green and glossy instead of turning brown. Five dried heads of *Rodgersia pinnata* 'Superba' repeat this ox-blood-red colour which is echoed again in the crenellated glass vase and silk cushion. Walls of palest apricot beige dictate the use of dark outline material for this group, and for this reason background and setting should always be consulted first.

The delicate sprays of skeletonized hibiscus leaves, sold by the packet, add grace to the design and soften the outline. These red leaves are wired individually with fine silver rose wire and then bound with a brown plastic self-adhesive tape called gutta-percha, a name derived from the Malay words for gum and tree.

A word about wire. Florist's wires are sold in standard lengths and thickness referred to as gauge. They should be blue-black and free from rust when purchased. This special wire bends at right angles caused by the annealling or tempering process used in its manufacture. Standard gauges go from 18, the strongest, to 26, the finest. The American equivalent is usually painted green, is slippery to handle and consequently not as easy to work with, but it does not corrode. Bundles in cut lengths vary from six inches to eighteen inches, but as I write all this is in the process of metrication and will be altered and doubtless reappear twice as expensive. Store in a dry place, wrapped in silver foil. Strong-gauge wires, hollow stems and slim garden canes all come in handy for extending short material on to false stems. This process is called 'mounting up'. Start at the tip with the smallest leaf and bind on to a 22-gauge wire with tape, adding leaves and wires to strengthen the main stem as you build up the spray. If each leaf has already been mounted on to a 22-gauge wire after it was first stitched with silver wire the process will flow more easily. The idea is to recreate a branching spray and once this process has been mastered it can be put to many uses, especially at Christmas time. All wires should be covered with tape and never ever should wires be twisted together. When garlands or swags are constructed, every item is wired and taped individually after the selection of the gauge of wire best suited to support each item. They are then bound with black or silver reel wire to cord in the case of loose garlands, or to stiff wire for more rigid shapes. Covering the foundation wire and individual items with tape helps enormously, for the binding wire has more to bite on to and items do not slip about.

Towards the centre of the decoration are grouped large poppy heads and a few glycerined leaves of loquat, *Eriobatrya japonica*. Large pressed leaves of *Hibiscus tiliaceus* consolidate the focal area, framing the dried heads of *Eryngium gigantium*, the latter saved from a fresh summer display. The steely involucre of Miss Willmott's Ghost still retains a soft blue tint. The loose covers of oyster-beige damask and a small head cushion repeat these colours and textures.

Decorations of this type may last many months – even years – but are of course a dust trap and need gentle cleaning from time to time. A hair-drier can be used at 'cold' to blow dust away. Glycerined foliage can be washed in tepid soapy water or sponged clean *in situ*. Over-dry materials can be revived in the steam from a boiling kettle or gently stiffened with a cool steam iron. Arrangements with such long-lasting qualities can be a real boon to the busy person. However, we all benefit from a change and I enjoy dismantling, grooming and rearranging mine with new materials when opportunity and fresh inspiration come along.

8 Christmas

Christmas decorations offer the greatest scope of any season to the flower arranger, for we allow ourselves the full gamut of materials including evergreens, fresh flowers, dried and preserved, gilded, glittered and even the artificial. Can it be because of this wide range that many decorations develop into a confused hotch-potch of mixed origins? As this is a book about growing and arranging flowers, I am limiting myself to fresh materials only. Whilst admiring ethereal effects with frost and glitter powders and fantasy creations for after dark, they do not come within the more specific terms of reference of this book. By all means create something different, but nothing refreshes the spirits quite like the simple beauty of glossy evergreens and a few fresh flowers. The busy person, and we all seem to get more frantic as Christmas approaches, will welcome artificial designs made well in advance and brought out like party dresses to dazzle at night. These never seem quite so exciting or glamorous by daylight, however – or is it that we feel a little jaded the morning after?

By tradition this is a time for renewing old friendships and giving hospitality to others, so let us begin with a welcome design for the door. The idea of a door or lintel decoration goes back to pre-Christian times, when cutting and decorating with evergreens was thought to bring good fortune and ward off evil spirits. Garlands of holly, ivy and mistletoe were used for pagan rites and were especially associated with the cult of Druidism. Perhaps in a landscape devoid of colour it seemed natural that the evergreens of the forest should symbolize new hope and new life as the winter solstice was celebrated. Our early Christian forefathers had the good sense to incorporate many of these ancient customs into their new religion, so even today we keep alive traditions possibly many thousands of years older than the birth of Christ.

Nowadays we can hang a bough of evergreen upon the door tied with ribbon to express to passers-by our greeting. This can be as simple or as elaborate as time and pocket will allow, but the type of door will dictate the style of decoration we create. I am lucky to live in a house which possesses the type of gate usually seen on Christmas cards. It replaces an older gate, is designed to fit an existing frame, and accords well with the antique lantern and wrought iron archway. The door is very plain and can take a large decoration without hindrance to those who pass through. Illuminated by a lantern, it suggests a welcome to all, strangers and friends alike, at this season of goodwill.

The foundation of the decoration consists of a shallow, plastic circle shaped like a trough or posy ring and sold by florists already fitted with Oasis. This is lightly moistened and then bound with narrow strips of polythene of the thinnest gauge. The bags used by dry cleaners make useful bandages if cut lengthways into three-inch-wide pieces. This protection is necessary because high winds and rains may give the decoration quite a battering and over-soak the foam base. If this superior type of foundation is not available, a wire wreath frame bound with soft moss is almost as good and much cheaper. Most florists stock frames ready mossed. Once again, the frame can be bound with polythene as it helps to prevent rust from wires and moisture marking the door. The frame used in Plate XV measures fifteen inches in diameter.

The foam or mossed frame can be decorated in a variety of ways, but as it is to hang out of doors in all weathers, natural materials look the most appropriate. An indoor version of dried, gilded leaves and fake fruits could be made up from all those tired pieces we had not the heart to dispose of in previous years. A good arranger has all the habits of a squirrel and, I hope, somewhere to store his or her hoard. It has been

XV Christmas door garland

said those with no attics have no past, and for the flower arranger her past is frequently her future! Looking through one's store of treasured things will help to rekindle the inspiration so often flagging when many pre-Christmas tasks demand attention.

One of the outstanding evergreens for Christmas is the blue form of the Colorado Spruce, *Picea pungens* 'Glauca', kindly supplied by a London-based florist friend. It lasts many weeks in water and at least until Twelfth Night out of water. First cut small sprigs of spruce or other evergreenery and sharpen the ends with a knife, inserting them through the polythene into the moss or foam so that they create an overlapping pattern. This can be varied by using single ivy leaves, holly and cupressus. If you can employ a colour-scheme the effect will be even better. My example keeps exclusively to blue-green and cream foliage using spruce, two ivies, *Hedera canariensis* 'Variegata' and *Hedera colchica* 'Dentato-variegata', *Cyclamen neapolitanum*, albino shoots of holly, *Ilex aquifolium* 'Silver Queen' and the reversed leaves of *Elaeagnus macrophylla*, included for their silvery lustre. The ivy, cyclamen and elaeagnus leaves are all wired with a 24-gauge wire which is stitched across the back centre vein and then doubled round the stem for support. Clusters of reindeer moss are added with wired pine cones. My only concession to the artificial is a few miniature red pomegranates interspersed amongst the foliage for added colour.

Because it is a large door a secondary grouping is added at the bottom of the circlet consisting of artificial apples, sprays of cotoneaster berries, lichen-covered larch twigs and large, imported Italian fir cones. The whole design is completed with four loops and two lavish tails of velvet ribbon. The asymmetrical placement of the water-repellent ribbon, balanced by the diagonal movement of the berries and twigs, counteracts the collective formality of the door, arch and railings.

An interesting supply of cut foliage is hard to come by at Christmas time and arrangers must grow their own to acquire a variety. Most florists' stock is limited to pittosporum, eucalyptus, ruscus and grevillea, plus the much abused Asparagus Fern, to set off the expensive forced flowers purchased at this time of year. There are a great many excellent shrubs we can grow to augment our displays and at the same time give bone structure to the garden. Broad, solid leaves for the centre of big designs are discussed in Chapter 1, but some of the lesser known ferns deserve a place in the arranger's garden. Some of these are evergreen and can be picked quite fresh even after snow and frost have flattened them. Those included in the decoration in Plate 1 bear witness to this as they were gathered in January. The majority enjoy a shady, cool place in the garden with plenty of leaf mould and humus present in the soil, plus room to display their leaf formation. However, some will grow in seemingly inhospitable crevices amongst stones or on old walls provided there is plenty of atmospheric moisture. Ferns belong to a primitive group of plants which do not bear flowers in the more accepted sense. They reproduce by spores or sori, usually borne on the underside of the leaf frond or occasionally in some species by separate fruiting fronds carried in the centre of the plant and adapted to this reproductive function. An example of this type of development is found in the Ostrich Plume Fern, *Matteuccia struthiopteris*. Most ferns seem to have diabolically difficult names, but don't be put off by such tongue-twisters for they are really beautiful things to grow. This fern has many Latin synonyms and also bears the common name of Shuttlecock Fern arising from the way the infertile fronds arrange themselves into handsome, upstanding whorls like overlapping feathers when fully expanded, grouped around a central crown of brown scales. In time this stump increases in size and rises like a short stem from wet ground. The fertile fronds are dark brown and covered with a fine powder of sori, irritating to sensitive skin but an interesting adjunct to dried and preserved decorations and persisting all winter. A close relation of this fern is the *Onoclea sensibilis*, a wildling of the swamps of the northern states of the USA and parts of Canada, where I have eaten the young, furled tips or Fiddle Heads as a vegetable – quite delicious, but a twinge of indigestion followed as I thought of my perseverance to establish a colony in my own garden. In both species the mature, infertile fronds press beautifully and should be gathered in July before they die down in autumn. They can be used naturally or lightly gilded and sprinkled with frost or glitter powder, the central midrib being strengthened with wire fixed with clear adhesive tape. A Christmas decoration of carefully pressed ferns and glycerined or dried grasses such as Quaking Grass, *Briza maxima*, and Hare's Tail Grass, *Lagurus ovatus*, treated in this way looks ethereal and far outshines the plastic counterparts which seek to imitate them.

Another graceful fern long established with me and illustrated in Figure 19 is the hardy Shield Fern, *Polystichum setiferum* 'Divisilobum'. There are various forms of Soft Shield Fern, but this is the most elegant to my mind. Tolerant of drier conditions, the evergreen fronds are arranged in a horizontal plane and grown with a light spiral twist from crown to tip. The entire stem is encased in brown, shaggy scales from which the individual fronds extend in a fine green filigree. Many forms of *P. setiferum* put forth plantlets from which they can be propagated and which add greatly to their interest in the garden or when arranged. My original plant of the plain *P. setiferum* is over fifty years old and once belonged to my grandmother who cultivated it as a pot plant.

The third in this illustrated trio is relatively new to me coming from the nursery of that great fern expert, Mr Reginald Kaye. The Buckler Ferns and Male Fern both belong to the genus *Dryopteris*; the majority are deciduous, but not so the beautiful *Dryopteris erythrosora*, from China and Japan. Why do the Orientals have all the best plants? The bold, broad leaves of this fern are evergreen and the young shoots are as arresting as any flower. They emerge as tiny shrimp-pink croziers, which change to a soft, rosy brown as they extend, a thing of great beauty. The underside of the mature frond bears scarlet spore capsules which show as small white scars on the upper surface. This is a rare plant but deserves wider cultivation. The Male Fern, *Dryopteris filix-mas*, is very common by comparison, but well worth growing as it tolerates most soil conditions, presses well and remains evergreen in sheltered positions, cohabiting with the Lady Fern, *Athyrium filix-femina*, if not actually enjoying conjugal bliss, for they belong to separate genera.

As cut material it is recommended practice to singe the cut ends of all ferns before soaking them in deep water. This is especially important for the hardy Maiden Hair Ferns, *Adiantum pedatum*, and the more tender *Adiantum venustum*. One unusual fern from my collection is the wavy-edged Hart's Tongue Fern, which glories in the name of *Phyllitis scolopendrium* 'Crispum'. It does not last well when cut, but gently pressed and then revived with a steam iron it is possible to regoffer its frills for use as dried material.

The dining-room is one of the focal areas of the house at Christmas time with the traditional dinner and other opportunities to savour special dishes and seasonal foods. The shops are full of imported fruits. They lend a colourful and exotic note to stores and markets and make ideal material for a decoration with their hint of richness expressed through colours and textures not easily found elsewhere, except in the more expensive imported flowers. A party gives a good excuse to create something lavish with the knowledge that all the ingredients of our display can later find their way into the kitchen or the dessert plate. This fact always helps to salve my conscience if I overspend on this type of decoration, but fruits are less expensive than flowers when their use is twofold.

The arrangement in Plate XVI is created on a mahogany breakfront sideboard. The background, dominated by the painting of Isabella, Duchess of Grafton, attributed to Sir Godfrey Kneller, acts as a dark foil for the

Figure 19

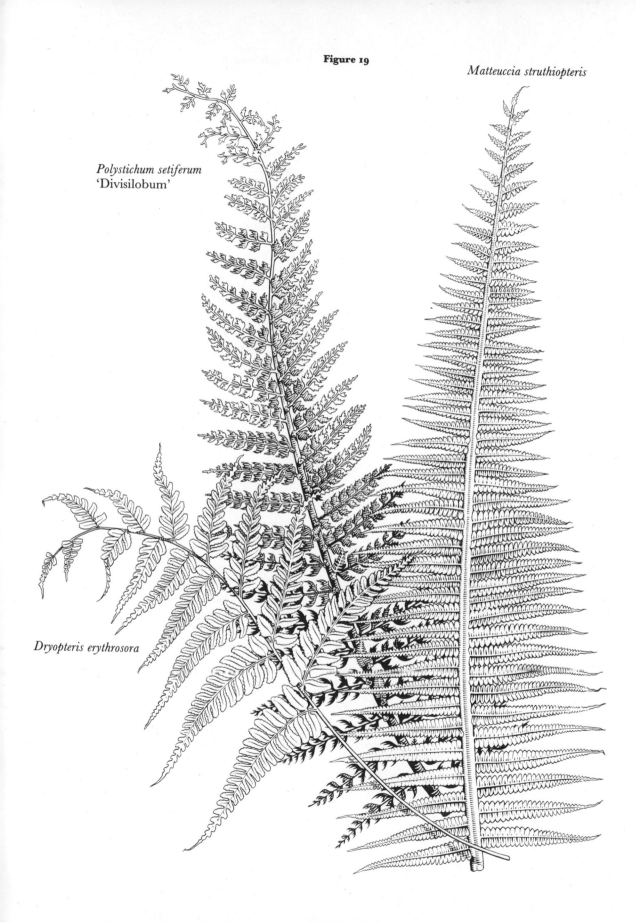

Matteuccia struthiopteris

Polystichum setiferum
'Divisilobum'

Dryopteris erythrosora

flowers, foliage and fruits. It is flanked by decanters of port and brandy which glow under the pools of light from French marble lamps. The symmetry of such a balanced and static grouping is deliberately broken by the openness of the decoration with its freedom of design. In creating a still-life composition we could occupy the entire sideboard, but the space will be needed for other accoutrements. The frame is set by the diameter of the tray and the sweep of the woman's arm. Just as the painter managed to create movement within the confines of the framed canvas, so must the arranger fit his or her decoration to the confines of the given space. I am always tempted to add that extra trail which would inevitably get trapped in the cutlery drawer. In any composition involving loose placements a tray is useful, for it holds all the items together and, one hopes, gently reminds the less observant guest that this is to look at and not to eat just yet. We all suffer from those who, like the fox in the fable, find the grapes too tempting.

The container, not visible, is a silver soup tureen doubling as a heated breakfast dish for bacon and eggs by the addition of an inner liner. This plate holds a full block of Oasis weighted underneath with a large pinholder. The pre-soaked Oasis and pinholder are strapped in place firmly with tape. Standing on an oval silver tray gives it importance and consolidates loose items of fruit and nuts. The design follows a gently asymmetric line dictated by the right arm of the Duchess and the flowing draperies of her dress. The first placements are of pure albino holly picked from the centre of a large bush of *Ilex aquifolium* 'Silver Queen' and contrasting in colour and shape with the glossy black clusters of wild privet, *Ligustrum vulgare*. The Kenyan pineapple is impaled on a tripod of wooden skewers which pass through the foam and on to the pinholder points ensuring stability. This luscious fruit symbolizes hospitality and as only the core is affected by the skewers it will be quite edible after the decoration is dismantled on Twelfth Night. Rosettes of purple Chinese

cabbage are placed in tubes of salted water, to prevent the attendant stale smell from developing; these tubes can be easily removed, emptied and refilled without disturbance to the whole. The colour of decorative kale and cabbage is intensified by light frosts but the outer damaged leaves have all been removed. To the right are sprays of red pepper, *Capsicum frutescens*, occasionally sold in sprays. These will last almost three months, ranging in colour through yellow, orange and red. Spraying out below these are the forced stalks and leaves of rhubarb, adding a bizarre note of colour. First condition the stems by recutting them and placing in deep, warm water, then leave to stand overnight. They do not last in foam but are gently placed under the block or to the side in free-standing water in the bottom of the dish. Because of the dark blue and red of the background all the foliage is chosen for its creamy whiteness, picking up the fabric colour of the lampshades. The ivy on the left is *Hedera helix* 'Marginata', which under the shelter of a vine produces enlarged trails of almost pure cream tinged with green. Towards the centre appear leaves of the lime-green *Hedera colchica* 'Paddy's Pride', a variety discussed later in this chapter and of outstanding merit. On the right are the pink-stemmed albino sprays of *Hedera canariensis* 'Variegata' and *Hedera colchica* 'Dentato-variegata', slightly more primrose than white. These sprays are devoid of chlorophyll so will not root once severed from the parent plant.

Other fruits consist of oranges for strong focal colour, lemons, apples and sweet peppers, *Capsicum annuum*, all impaled on clean wooden skewers. Avoid the green-painted variety as these will discolour the flesh and render the fruit useless for eating up later in a fruit salad. Cobs of decorative Indian corn, *Zea mays*, peep out on the right. The North American summer and fall are more conducive to the maturing of this crop than the British, but once ripened and stripped of the outer husks it lasts indefinitely if carefully stored. Green and purple Muscat grapes flow over the gallery of the tray, adding an opulent note in contrast to the smooth whiteness of the patty-pan squash, *Cucurbita pepo* 'Melopepo'. The latter is delicious boiled and mashed with butter.

The flowers are added once the fruit is arranged. Care should be taken to ensure that the fruits stand proud of the moist foam, relying on each other and their skewers for support. The flower and leaf stems pass between them into the foam, which should be topped up daily. Rusty red anemone-centred chrysanthemums are the old fashioned variety 'Raymond Molesdale', combined with strawberry-pink spray carnations and a few magenta anemones. I enjoy combinations of this kind, giving such scope for the juxtapositioning of fruit, vegetables and allied subjects.

Several good ivies are used in this last illustration which brings us to my conclusive section on winter foliage. It is a pity that ivy has acquired such an undeservedly bad reputation for it includes some of the most beautiful of all climbing evergreen plants. Perhaps it is because of its vigorous growth and propensity to cling that it is unpopular. The idea that it is parasitic to trees is without truth although it can strangle its host if left unchecked. The forceful roots will in time crack open stone and dislodge mortar, but then so will other plants if neglected. Kept under proper control – not a difficult task for a flower arranger – the variegated varieties are indispensable decorators both indoors and out. The all-green forms must be cut back ruthlessly in mid-March before they develop into a block of flats for nesting birds. This pruning encourages the ivies to reclothe themselves with new leaves during the summer. It is useless, however, to pick this new growth for it quickly wilts. I am not tempted by it during the growing season except to gloat occasionally on seeing some well marked spray developing. It is not until deciduous leaves turn colour that I become aware of all the beauty that has been maturing unobtrusively.

There are so many good varieties to choose from that I must limit myself to three of outstanding merit with but scant mention of a

few other good clones. All are propagated by climbing or terminal shoots. When scandent these shoots possess aerial roots adapted to cling to any available surface. These adventitious roots will not immediately feed the severed spray. Place the cutting in a small bottle of dark glass two-thirds full of water (root formation is inhibited by daylight), and wait patiently. Feeding roots will emerge, especially in the humid area below the bottle neck and above the water line. In time a little soil can be added to feed the cutting and prepare it for its move to a plant pot of compost. Outdoor cuttings can be heeled in below a shady wall or dibbled into pots of cutting compost in a frame or greenhouse. All ivies are painfully slow to get started and anyone with itchy snippers will simply have to curb their desire for a year or two. Patience will be well rewarded, for established plants grow rapidly, throwing out plenty of material for picking. If you desire a bushy non-climbing plant take a flowering shoot as a cutting – it will grow into a bushy non-climbing shrub with larger entire leaves and bear flower heads. Ivy rarely flowers until it has exhausted the limits of its climbing space. The green flowers are not its main attraction for, blooming in late autumn, they pass unnoticed, pollinated by flies and late blue bottles. The green berries eventually turn black and persist in clusters until April. I recall arranging for Mrs Fish wild ivy berries and their cornelian-red leaves with the curious green and velvet black flowers of the Snake's Head, *Hermodactylus tuberosus*, a combination she approved. Mrs Fish loved ivies and gave me many cuttings. We were in high glee that day, having each acquired a cutting of a beautiful large-leaved ivy at that time new to us. It originated from the garden of Mrs Cecil Pope at Dorchester and had been carried off by us after the meeting of the Sherborne Flower Club. I later saw this variety in southern Ireland and in the garden of Mrs Beth Chatto. It enjoys the name of 'Paddy's Pride', but whether it has sported from *Hedera colchica* 'Dentata', which it resembles, or *Hedera helix* or even *Hedera hibernica*, accepting the premise that this is a separate species, it is difficult to say. Disentangling ivy names can be a problem. I regret I never gave a piece to the late Mrs Sybil Emberton for she would have classified it with her accustomed clarity.

The leaves are heart-shaped, entire and attractively marbled with lime green over mid-green, bronzed at the tips in winter. Painfully slow to start, it eventually will cover a big area clothing a north wall or some unwanted eyesore. It heads my list as a first-rate plant and is faithfully illustrated by Charles Stitt in Figure 20 in company with two others that share this personal accolade.

Hedera colchica 'Dentata' is one of the largest-leaved species, supplying enormous pedestal sprays and tough individual leaves. It is the variegated form which we more often see, *Hedera colchica* 'Dentato-variegata'. Less massive but still robust, the heart-shaped leaves are slightly toothed, cream to primrose yellow over-splashed with central green and grey-green on brown stems. Grown over a low wall or balustrade, it will put forth well poised sprays free from unsightly aerial roots, and good for cutting. Individually the larger leaves make excellent focal material as do the flower shoots, and it occasionally presents us with distinctive entirely cream leaves.

Hedera helix is referred to as English Ivy in the United States and is still enjoying the post-war rage as a pot plant, popularized by Constance Spry in the late forties through Messrs Tom Rochford and Sons Ltd. Ten years later I survived my entire National Service with one small spray of a small-leaved form, then called 'Chicago', secreted in a miniature liqueur bottle. It eluded every kit inspection and after two years of hydroponic existence had developed a fine root system. I called it 'Sanity' as it symbolized a link between me and the world of gardens from which I was temporarily separated. I still feel a twinge of guilt that it never travelled to my present garden to find a fitting resting place.

The variegated ivy which most closely resembles *Hedera helix* 'Chicago Variegata' is now called 'Silver Queen' or 'Marginata'. The leaves vary enormously according to its growth position. When in contact with soil it runs and roots, staying quite compact and small, but when on the ascent into a sheltered corner the triangular leaves treble in size, elegantly arranged in a fine mosaic, each lobe sharply pointed and margined with white overlaid with central green. These delectable out-of-reach bits are hard to detach entire, but can be coveted all winter. This ivy scorches in strong sunshine and, like other thin-leaved variegated varieties, requires sheltered shade.

There is a lot of pleasure to be derived from a collection of ivies; I can boast of twenty-two varieties, but rather than claim a horticultural zoo, one of everything, I will mention only a few useful cultivars for floral work.

Hedera helix 'Gold Heart' is also known as 'Jubilee', the small, mid-green leaves splashed with central yellow on rosy-pink stems. It tends to revert to all-green in deep shade and I find it stiff to arrange. More promising is 'Gold Child', a new arrival. The small leaves have all the helix qualities at their daintiest, and the colour is arresting – citrus yellow with a central greenness, on pointed leaves. It appears quite hardy against a sheltered wall and is starting to scramble and climb. Similar in leaf but with a more elongated central point is 'Sagittaefolia', the Arrow Head Ivy. This makes a good cascader if sited in a bed or window box where it can flow downwards. For irregular crimped and curly leaves 'Cristata' arouses interest: fresh green, it looks like parsley at a distance, but half-starved or dry in a pot it turns a distressing coppery pink, just right for the jaundiced eye of the flower arranger. I have enjoyed several pots standing out in stone jars and treated this way in summer.

One of the most popular of ivies as a house plant is *Hedera canariensis* 'Variegata', once known as 'Gloire de Marengo'. It has a reputation for tenderness out of doors. I have plants in several different aspects and all come through hard frosts unscathed. Occasionally

Figure 20

Hedera helix 'Marginata'

Hedera colchica 'Dentato-variegata'

Hedera colchica 'Paddy's Pride'

sudden sunshine on frozen foliage will do harm, but cold, dry spring winds are the real culprit. The leaves are edged with white and overlaid with grey and grey-green prettily flushed with pink as a protection against the cold. I welcome the occasional stem that reverts to all-green on one big expanse I have, because these larger leaves have a unique burnished sheen, good for winter pedestals and complementary to the variegated sprays. This is by no means an exhaustive description, but will form a basis for a good collection of easy, space-earning plants.

In conclusion, may I hope that you will have shared some of my enthusiasms, especially for foliage. I shall be more than satisfied if I have been able to introduce my readers to some plants new to their acquaintance, to enhance their gardens and to provide scope for occasional cutting. I hope that the many flower arrangers, whose support and encouragement I value so much, will feel inspired to grow a greater variety of plants. Do not be afraid to develop your own individual style of arranging. To those who grow plants only for garden decoration, I hope I have been able to offer some suggestions for decorative plant associations, and perhaps to engender a better understanding of why we flower arrangers can cut from our plants without compunction.

Seek out only those things which are beautiful and distinctive to your eye, always remembering that one simple thing of quality, well used, will far outweigh a dozen items of inferior origin. I hope that in your searchings you will, by happy chance, make many discoveries, as I have done in the compilation of this book.

List of suppliers

Bulbs

Walter Blom & Son Ltd., Coombelands Nurseries, Leavesden, Watford, Herts.
Broadleigh Gardens, Barr House, Bishops Hull, Taunton, Somerset.
Orpington Nurseries Co., Ltd., Rocky Lane, Gatton Park, Reigate, Surrey.
Van Tubergen Ltd., Willow Bank Wharf, Ranelagh Gardens, Fulham, London SW6.
Wallace & Barr Ltd., The Nurseries, Marden, Kent.

Clematis

Fisk's Clematis Nursery, Westleton, Nr. Saxmundham, Suffolk.
Pennell & Sons Ltd., Princess Street, Lincoln.
Treasures of Tenbury Ltd., Tenbury Wells, Worcs.

Ferns

Reginald Kaye Ltd., Waithman Nurseries, Silverdale, Carnforth, Lancs.

Herbaceous Plants

Beth Chatto, Unusual Plants, White Barn House, Elmstead Market, Colchester, Essex.
Margery Fish Nursery, East Lambrook Manor, South Petherton, Somerset.
Great Dixter Nurseries (Christopher Lloyd), Northiam, Sussex.
Mrs D. Horne, Timberland, Lincoln.
Kelways Nurseries (John A. Lloyd), Langport, Somerset. (Irises and peonies.)
R. Poland, Brook House Nursery, Highbrook Road, Ardingly, Sussex.
Treasures of Tenbury Ltd., Tenbury Wells, Worcs.
Treseders' Nurseries (Truro) Ltd., Moresk Road, Truro, Cornwall. (Especially for mild climates.)
Mrs Desmond Underwood, Colchester, Essex. (Pinks and grey foliage plants.)

Roses

E. B. LeGrice (Roses) Ltd., Roseland Nurseries, North Walsham, Norfolk.
John Mattock Ltd., Nuneham Courtenay, Oxford.
Sunningdale Nurseries Ltd., The Waterer Group, Windlesham, Surrey.

Seeds

Sutton & Sons Ltd., Torquay, Devon.
Thompson & Morgan Ltd., London Road, Ipswich.

Trees and Shrubs

A. J. T. Bayles, Grey Timbers, Chapple Road, Bovey Tracey, Devon. (For eucalpytus.)
Bodnant Garden Nursery, Tal-y-Cafyn, Colwyn Bay, N. Wales.
Hillier & Sons, Winchester, Hampshire.
Notcutt's Nurseries Ltd., Woodbridge, Suffolk.
R. V. Roger Ltd., The Nurseries, Pickering, Yorks.
Roseacre Garden Centre, Kidderminster Road South, West Hagley, Worcs.
John Scott & Co., The Royal Nurseries, Merriott, Somerset.

Florists

F. H. Ward, 2 Clifford Street, York.
Robert Day & Co. Ltd., 4 Ladbroke Grove, London W11.

Bibliography

Bean, W. J.,
Trees and Shrubs Hardy in the British Isles, vols. 1 and 2 (John Murray Ltd, eighth edition revised 1976)

Emberton, Sybil C.,
Garden Foliage for Flower Arrangement (Faber & Faber Ltd, London, 1968)
Shrub Gardening for Flower Arrangement (Faber & Faber Ltd, London, 1965)
Growing Plants for Flower Arrangement (Royal Horticultural Society [Wisley Handbook 20], London, 1975)

Ingwersen, Will,
Classic Garden Plants (Hamlyn Publishing Group Ltd, 1975)

Kaye, Reginald,
Hardy Ferns (Faber & Faber Ltd, 1968)

Keble Martin, W.,
The Concise British Flora in Colour (Ebury Press and Michael Joseph, 1969)

Lloyd, Christopher,
Foliage Plants (Wm. Collins Sons & Co. Ltd, London, 1973)
The Well Tempered Garden (Wm. Collins Sons & Co. Ltd, 1970)

Royal Horticultural Society,
Dictionary of Gardening (second edition, 1974, supplement 1969, Oxford University Press, London)

Synge, Patrick M.,
Collins Guide to Bulbs (Wm. Collins Sons & Co. Ltd, London, 1971)

Thomas, Graham Stuart,
Perennial Garden Plants (J. M. Dent & Sons Ltd, London, 1976)
Old Shrub Roses (J. M. Dent & Sons Ltd, London, last reprinted 1966)
Shrub Roses of Today (J. M. Dent & Sons Ltd, London, last reprinted 1963
Colour in the Winter Garden (J. M. Dent & Sons Ltd, London, last reprinted 1967)
Plants for Ground Cover (J. M. Dent & Sons Ltd, London, 1970)

Underwood, Mrs Desmond,
Grey and Silver Plants (Wm. Collins Sons & Co. Ltd, London, 1971)

Index

*Page numbers in italics refer to the pages on which plants are
illustrated*